NO
MERE
MORTALS

NO
MERE
MORTALS

Marriage for People
Who Will Live Forever

TOBY J.
SUMPTER

Published by Canon Press
P.O. Box 8729, Moscow, Idaho 83843
800.488.2034 | www.canonpress.com

Cover design by James Engerbretson
Interior design by Samuel Dickison

Printed in the United States of America.

20 21 22 23 24   5 4 3 2 1

CONTENTS

For Jenny

Pro patribus tuis erunt filii tibi
Pones eos principes in universa terra

INTRODUCTION

So you are married. Congratulations. Cheers! Well done.

Maybe you just got married and you're wanting to make sure the cement dries and the foundation is plumb. Or, maybe you've been married for many years now and you're looking for some retooling, a refresher, a little brush-up on what this whole marriage thing is. Or maybe your marriage is in trouble and you're looking for help. Or maybe you aren't quite married yet—you're just engaged and looking to start off your new life together on the right path. No matter which of these you are, this book begins with our only hope for a Christian marriage: Jesus Christ. Then it walks through some of the most important principles for building or rebuilding a strong foundation and walking together with your spouse in the Lord.

If you aren't even engaged yet, feel free to read this book, but just be prepared for the fact that I'm not covering a whole bunch of stuff about dating and courtship and how to know if he's the one or she's the one and how to maneuver through the various relationship minefields. This book assumes that you put a ring on it—or at the very least that you've made up your mind and agreed to take the plunge.

True confessions: the basic shape of this book has grown out of many years of premarital counseling. The material here has been significantly expanded for the entire marriage gambit, but if my language occasionally slips into premarital counseling mode, now you know why. I also need to note that I have had the great honor of ministering in close proximity to Pastor Douglas Wilson for many years, marinating in his books and sermons and Bible studies. I have tried to note when I'm sure I'm repeating something he has said, but anyone who is familiar with his work will recognize his pervasive influence in what follows. And if you haven't read his family books, I cannot recommend them to you strongly enough, especially *Reforming Marriage* and *Federal Husband*.

So whether you have been married for a while, or just got married, or even just got engaged, I hope what follows is a helpful summary of some of the most basic biblical principles for Christian marriage, applied to our modern day. We will begin this book with a couple of topical chapters, and then work through a number of verses from Ephesians 5 and 1 Peter 3 before closing with a few more topical chapters. That's the basic structure, but before we get down to brass tacks, let me sketch you something of a biblical picture of marriage.

In recent decades, we have essentially reduced marriage to a permanent roommate situation with sexual benefits. Our assumptions about the purpose and mission of the family make the biblical commands seem obtuse or oppressive. As my friend Pastor Chris Wiley points out, when it comes to discussing the leadership of the man and the submission of the woman, it can sound like the Bible is insisting that the man controls the TV remote—since for many people, what they're going to watch seems like the biggest decision that needs to be made in the home.

But the biblical picture of the family is something far more glorious, far more dangerous—something more like a nuclear reactor. If moderns balk at the Old Testament's death penalty for adultery (Lev. 20:10) or the death penalty for a rebellious son (Deut. 21:18-21), this is not because we are highly evolved and enlightened moderns, but rather because we have such a low view of marriage and family. The Bible has such severe penalties for the destruction of a home because of the resulting destructive fallout. The Bible says that God hates divorce because of how it covers one's garment with violence (Mal. 2:16), and we nod naively, still thinking that the Old Testament penalties seem sort of harsh and barbaric. Barbaric? For the last fifty years, the sexual revolution has championed everything from pornography to homosexuality to even the beginnings of full-blown pederasty, and the price for that perversion party has been the blood of over sixty million babies and counting. And we think God was kind of harsh and barbaric? No, we are the harsh and barbaric ones.

Even the most ardent defender of Second Amendment rights has to have had second thoughts on the question of whether every private citizen ought to have access to nukes. I mean, the usual claim is that the citizenry ought to have the means to resist tyrannical governments. And, well, if the government has nukes, shouldn't the citizens? But those stakes are extremely high, and an accident would have far-reaching consequences. And suddenly, the most dyed-in-the-wool libertarian wonders if there ought to be at least a little barbed wire around that catastrophe waiting to happen. Bring this back to the family: God has placed His image in man, and every human being bears the imprint of the eternal, infinite, sovereign God. There is nothing in all the world quite so powerful as people. And therefore, the place where people are *made* is basically a nuclear reactor, and the stakes are much higher than we realize. We are making people who will live forever, people with souls that will grow into the greatest horrors or most glorious beings.[1] And those people will go on to build and invent and create and love and fight and dance and make more people. We are in the process of setting off reactions that will do great good or great harm.

The good news of the gospel is that the All-Powerful, All-Sufficient God has come into this world in the person of His Son in order to set off another nuclear reaction, a

---

1. See C.S. Lewis's *The Weight of Glory* (New York: Macmillan: 1980), 18-19.

reaction of blessing that is in the process of commandeering all of our familial reactions and filling this world with God's life and light.

Too often we misunderstand the words of Jesus regarding the future of marriage. We hear Him say that we will not marry or be given in marriage in Heaven, and we think He was saying that we ought not think so highly of marriage. But that cannot be the case since the whole Bible ends in a marriage, the Marriage Supper of the Lamb. So it's simply not true to say that there is no marriage in Heaven. There is at least one marriage in Heaven, the marriage of the Lamb. Sure, our earthly marriages are transfigured into something far more glorious, but the point is not at all that marriage is not such a big deal. Rather, the point is that our earthly problems will not be problems in Heaven. And that is because all of our weddings are pointing to the Great Wedding.

Paul says in Ephesians that our earthly marriages point to the Great Marriage, and he says it's a great mystery. Now we need not buy into the Roman Catholic view that makes marriage a sacrament, but neither do we need to back away from Paul's language in the slightest. It really is a great mystery: a glorious mystery, a powerful mystery. From Adam and Eve to Abraham and Sarah to Boaz and Ruth to Solomon and the Shulamite to Hosea and Gomer to Joseph and Mary, God has been revealing a great mystery, something glorious about the way the world is, about the way God Himself is, about Christ and the Church.

Getting marriage right has implications far beyond the home. The officers of the Church are to be men who rule their own households well, fathers in the Church (1 Tim. 3, Tit. 1, 1 Cor. 3). Civil magistrates are to be foster fathers and nursing mothers (Is. 49:23). Our English Old Testament closes with the promise of Malachi to "turn the hearts of fathers to their children, and the hearts of children to their fathers, lest I come and strike the earth with a curse" (Mal. 4:6, NKJV). Do we want our land blessed, our businesses blessed, our churches blessed, and our public squares blessed? Then we need to get marriage right, which is to say we need to get family right. Christ died on the cross to take the curse of sin and death, in order to turn the hearts of fathers and sons, in order to heal families, in order that a sinful man (an immortal soul) and a sinful woman (an immortal soul) might make vows in a church before witnesses (immortal souls), in full assurance that God's blessing rests upon them and will follow them and their children (immortal souls, all) all the days of their life (and forever).

CHAPTER 1

MARRY IN THE LORD

WHAT is your testimony?

Tell the story of how you came to know Jesus Christ as your Lord and Savior. If you grew up in a Christian family or in the Church, tell that story. Were there particular moments in your life growing up where you have experienced God's grace in your life? Where you came to understand more fully what it meant to be a child of God? Were there particular seasons of growth or repentance or doubt or rebellion? If you grew up outside the faith, tell how the Lord drew you to Himself.

Go ahead, I'll wait. Take turns. Tell your story out loud.

After sharing your testimonies, take turns answering one more question: If someone asked you *why* you are a Christian, what would you say? How would you summarize the good news of Jesus in one or two sentences? What does it mean that you are a follower of Jesus?

Read 1 Corinthians 15:1–10. Notice the final couple of verses where Paul summarizes his testimony: "Last of all, as to one untimely born, he appeared also to me. For I am least of the apostles, unworthy to be called an apostle, because I persecuted the church of God. But by the grace of God I am what I am, and his grace toward me was not in vain. On the contrary, I worked harder than any of them, though it was not I, but the grace of God that is with me" (1 Cor. 15:8–10, ESV).

Whether you have known Jesus all of your life or only more recently experienced the grace of God, His grace is never in vain. It's never impotent or weak or futile. His grace is powerful. Sometimes His grace can seem more amazing to us—like when God saves someone like Paul on his way to Damascus breathing threats against the followers of Jesus, absolutely convinced that they are enemies of God, and then BAM! God knocks them down and radically changes them. Maybe you or someone you know was in high-handed rebellion, addicted to drugs or alcohol, sexually promiscuous, suicidal, or just full of plain old vanilla devil-pride, and God saved them. Those are glorious stories, glorious testimonies of God's grace.

But there are no boring stories of grace. When God grips us as young children and preserves us from some of the most ugly manifestations of sin in the world, that too is God's amazing grace. With true and humble gratitude may we say we have a "boring testimony"—in the sense that we've never gone through a period of prolonged rebellion, joined a biker gang, robbed a bank, or partied like pagans. Because of our parents' faithfulness and God's grace, our testimony can seem gloriously boring. And thank God for those testimonies.

But properly speaking, God's grace is never actually boring, never truly mundane, never weak. It's always high octane. This is because nobody deserves God's grace, and while God's grace is truly, wonderfully free, salvation is not free. Your salvation, and my salvation, was terribly expensive. Christ purchased us with His precious blood. "You are not your own, for you were bought with a price" (1 Cor. 6:19–20, ESV). No one comes to God with a minor debt or with a little sin problem. Everyone is dead in Adam, each a lifeless corpse, enslaved to sin and death and Satan—whether you were three years old or thirteen years old or thirty years old. Every one of us owed a debt we could never pay. Every one of us had a *just* death sentence hanging over our heads. And every one of us was redeemed by the precious blood of Jesus: "you were ransomed from the futile ways inherited from your forefathers, not with perishable things such as silver or gold, but with the precious blood of Christ, like that of a lamb without blemish or spot" (1 Pet. 1:18–19, ESV).

No testimony should be boring because every testimony is about the most precious, most valuable thing in all the world: our Jesus, our Savior, our Redeemer, and His blood that washes us clean and grants us the gift of everlasting life.

So let me challenge you: if you aren't used to telling your testimony, or if you gave a glib, two-sentence testimony (e.g., "My parents were Christians, and I grew up in the Church and that's about it"), stop here and try again. Think back on your life. Where have you experienced God's grace? Have you witnessed answered prayer? Have you seen Him at work in reconciling broken relationships? Have you known His forgiveness? You *should* be able to tell stories of these things. And if you really can't talk about God's grace in your life, let me challenge you to seriously consider whether you really *are* a Christian.

It's not enough to have Christian parents. It's not enough to have been baptized. It's not enough to grow up in the Church. Do you know Christ? Do you know that the Holy Spirit dwells in you? One can be a Christian outwardly, formally, but not a true Christian inwardly (cf. Rom. 2:28–29). The Jews *did* have Abraham as their covenantal father, and they had the genealogical paperwork to prove it. But they actually had the devil as their real father (Jn. 8:44). Paul writes to the Corinthians, people he addresses as "sanctified in Christ Jesus," and says, "Examine yourselves, to see whether you are in the faith. Test yourselves. Or do you not realize this about yourselves, that Jesus Christ is in you?—unless indeed you fail to meet the test!" (2 Cor. 13:5, ESV).

A true Christian has not only been baptized on the outside and professed faith outwardly, but a true Christian has also had his heart washed clean by the blood of Christ and has been born again by the renewal of the Holy Spirit (Heb. 10:22, Tit. 3:5). This doesn't mean that you need to have seen a miraculous vision or spoken in tongues or had some kind dramatic emotional experience. But there should be fruit in your life—the fruit of the Spirit (Gal. 5:22–23, ESV). Do you see evidence of the Spirit's work in your life—convicting you of sin, conforming you to the image of Christ, causing you to grow in love for God and your neighbor more and more as the months and years go by?

This is actually an enormously important point to make at the beginning of a book about marriage, because the Bible is incredibly clear that Christians are only to marry other Christians, true believers in Christ. "You shall not intermarry with them, giving your daughters to their sons or taking their daughters for your sons, for they would turn away your sons from following me, to serve other gods. Then the anger of the LORD would be kindled against you, and he would destroy you quickly" (Deut. 7:3–4, ESV). And Paul makes a similar point in the New Covenant: "Do not be unequally yoked with unbelievers. For what partnership has righteousness with lawlessness? Or what fellowship has light with darkness?" (2 Cor. 6:14, ESV). And likewise, while a Christian should seek to preserve a marriage that already exists with a non-believer, if the non-believer departs, the Christian is not under bondage. In this case, or when a spouse dies, a Christian may remarry, but "only in the Lord" (1 Cor. 7:39).

In the early Church, one of the slanders the pagans spread about the Christians was that they practiced incest—intermarrying between brothers and sisters. Of course this was not true at all, but the slander grew out of the Christian commitment to only marrying other Christians. Going all the way back to the Song of Songs, even Solomon referred to his spouse as his "sister" (Song 4:9–12, 5:1). If you would not marry an unbeliever, why would you date or court an unbeliever? If you would not marry an unbeliever, why would you flirt with an unbeliever? Why would you keep up an overly friendly familiarity with an unbeliever if he or she is not even an option? Christians should be known for their commitment to marry only in the Lord, only in the family of God. I know I said this was a book for married people, not a book for people courting or dating, but I couldn't help myself. Some things just need saying.

A little further on this track before we move on … maybe you're thinking this has all gotten pretty deep and introspective. "Shouldn't we just take a compatibility test or something?" Well, actually, that is sort of what we're doing. The very first item on the list for compatibility for Christians is salvation in Christ. Non-Christians certainly can get married, and they really are married, since marriage is not just a thing for Christians. It's a creational institution for the good of all humans and human society. But Christians are commanded to marry "in the Lord" because when a man or woman comes to know Jesus, so much of who they are is affected, changed, and transformed. Our priorities are completely different. What motivates us is different. We have a new set of desires and goals, and in Jesus, we have been given a very specific *mission*. There are so many good things that are different about a man and a woman: different family backgrounds, different customs, different cultures, different tastes, interests, hobbies, and preferences, not to mention the wonderful sexual differences between a man and a woman. To try to fit a man and a woman together who have a different reason for living, a different fundamental motivation for what they do—this is a recipe for disaster, disappointment, and heartbreak. And there is no shortage of marital train wrecks documenting this sad reality.

Yes, you might have collected stamps or loved skiing or been a pretty good singer before you were a Christian, but even those skills or gifts or hobbies are reoriented to Christ when you become a Christian. Before, they may have been distractions, idols, covers for insecurity, but in Jesus they become gifts to enjoy, gifts to share, and somehow, we pray, they become part of our sacrifice of praise, spiritual acts of worship to our Creator and Savior. And if this is true for hobbies and pastimes, how much more so does it affect our vocational, educational, and familial aspirations and dreams? How do you decide which job to take? How do you organize your finances? Do you value children? Are you committed to fruitfulness in the marriage bed? Do you share a biblical understanding of the role of husband and wife? Do you share standards of fidelity and purity? Is it ever acceptable to view pornography? How will you discipline your children? How will you educate them? Will your boys and girls be raised differently according to their biological sex? Why? Does it matter?

In order to begin answering these questions, you must have a *standard*, a rule for life. This is why it is of the utmost importance that you marry someone who shares that foundational (re)orientation to Christ and His Word, someone who understands that Jesus is Lord of every square inch of your life, someone who is just as committed as you are to taking up the cross of Christ and following Him in obedience wherever He leads. Christians are committed to obey whatever the Bible says about finances, children, sex, vocation, and everything else. In other words, a true Christian is someone who has surrendered in principle. Whatever the Bible says, that's what we are committed to—our whole marriage long.

The apostle Paul describes what it's like to be a Christian this way: "I have been crucified with Christ; it is no longer I who live, but Christ lives in me; and the life which I now live in the flesh I live by faith in the Son of God, who loved me and gave Himself for me" (Gal. 2:20, ESV). Do you resonate with this? Do you know what Paul means?

Knowing the love of Christ goes all the way down into our deepest desires, our identities as men and women, as human beings made in God's image who are now being renewed into the image of Christ. We no longer live; now Christ lives in us. Now whatever we do, we do it *to the glory of God* (1 Cor. 10:31)—which is to say we are committed to obeying Christ. Given God's love, God's grace, God's goodness pouring over us, we want to live our lives as living sacrifices of praise. Why? Because He is worthy. He is our Lord, our Master, and we obey Him in everything because He saved us from sin, death, and Satan.

Our hearts burn within us with gratitude, with joy, with gladness, with relief. Our debts have all been paid. Our hearts are clean. And by the grace of God, we have been sent out into the world to fill it with His goodness and glory. He made the world and filled it with gifts, and He has always intended for men and women made in His image to take those gifts and build upon them, to be fruitful and multiply and fill the earth with garden-cities full of good food and fine wine, creative technology and industry, inspiring arts and architecture, with excellent and sacrificial care for the weak, the sick, the elderly, the disabled, not to mention courageous service in politics, economics, education, zoology, and tourism. And everywhere else I left out.

The gift of Christian marriage is the gift of friendship and an enormous help in this mission of following Jesus. There is a biblical ordering in God's assignments to men and women respectively; they are oriented to one another and to their various vocations in different ways (more on that later). But there is also a foundational discipleship-mutuality in this. When two Christians marry, they are first of all brother and sister in Christ, and God knows exactly what He's doing with both of them. His ultimate goal for both of them is Christ-likeness, and marriage is one of the most objective places where we can speak with confidence about what God is up to. He is saying you need this particular woman with all her quirks and peculiarities and gifts in order to grow up into the likeness and maturity of Christ. And *you* need this particular man with all of his unique quirks and peculiarities and gifts in order to grow up into the likeness and maturity of Jesus. By God's design, Christian marriage is one of the ordinary means of sanctification.

So you want a Christian marriage? We begin here. We begin with your testimony, with your story of God's grace, with your identity firmly fixed in Jesus Christ, with this shared commitment. You are not your own. You were bought with a price. You belong to Jesus. You have been born again to a new and living hope. You are on a mission of seeking glory and honor and immortality (Rom. 2:7). Jesus is your Lord and Master. So this whole thing is not really about you. It's about Him. It's about His plan, His mission in this world.

Most marital problems can be traced to problems here. Sometimes you thought your spouse was a Christian, sometimes one spouse becomes a Christian later in life, or sometimes very little time or effort has been spent explicitly anchoring your marriage in Christ. And one or both spouses are consciously or unconsciously pursuing their own mission, their own plans, and no wonder there is conflict. If you want your marriage to be blessed, it needs to line up with what Jesus is doing. You need His mission to be your mission. Therefore, His Word must shape everything about your plan. You want to live for Him *together*. Right?

QUESTIONS FOR DISCUSSION

1. *Why are there not really any boring testimonies—even if you grew up in the faith?*

2. *What's the difference between someone who is a Christian outwardly and a true Christian who is also one inwardly?*

3. *What does the Bible say about Christians marrying non-Christians (Deut. 7:3–4, 2 Cor. 6:14, 1 Cor. 7:39)?*

4. *Why is it so important for husband and wife to have a shared standard for morality? And what is that standard for Christians?*

5. *How do Christians do everything to the glory of God? What does that actually mean practically—how do you know for sure you're doing it?*

CHAPTER 2

RIGHTLY ORDERED
LOVE LIFE

WE began with your testimony and your life in Christ because this is the most significant thing about you. It goes all the way to your core. It is more significant than the family you were born into. It is more significant than your past sins and mistakes (thank God!). And it orients your goals, priorities, standards, and mission for the future.

In other words, even though marriage certainly is one of the most significant moments and decisions of your life (and it really is!), being found in Christ, being born again, belonging to Him is *more* important, *more* significant.

On your wedding day, tons about you changes. It's true. A woman takes her husband's name. A man becomes responsible before God for his wife. You have to learn to live together. What you have taken for granted about many things in life, like how to fold socks or how to organize the pantry or when to get up in the morning or how to prioritize your budget—some or all of that changed. The day before your wedding, you were a single man or a single woman, and the day after your wedding, you were a husband or a wife. You had become one flesh. You had formed a new family. You changed, and many things in your life changed. Like kids for example. They will change (or already have changed) you even more.

But here's the thing: despite the massive, monumental changes that occurred (or will occur) after your wedding, there is something even more massive, even more fundamental that will *never* change. On the day *before* your wedding, you were a son or daughter of the King, beloved of God, purchased by the blood of Jesus, secure in His firm grasp forever. And the day *after* your wedding, you were still that blood-bought child of God, saved for eternity. That identity can never change, shift, or be affected in the slightest.

And this is so important. You need to understand this deep in your bones, because many marital problems arise from misunderstanding this. People say that their wife or husband "completes" them. They say they are lost without their spouse. They say there was a hole in their heart without them. And there is a sense in which that is true. I get that. Love is like that. And I thank God for it. But there is another sense in which those sentiments are actually all wrong. There's a sense in which those sentiments can be pure idolatry. In other words, if you are placing all your hopes on marriage, if you think that being Mr. Husband or Mrs. Wife or finding Mr. or Mrs. "Right" is going to "complete" you and fulfill all your deepest longings and desires, I've got news for you.

I don't mean to be the pessimist or the anti-romantic. I love my wife, and I can't imagine life without her. But knowing Jesus Christ means that my identity is rooted first and foremost in *Him*. In fact, Jesus says that we cannot follow Him rightly unless we are willing to give up our dearest loves: "If anyone comes to me and does not hate his own father and mother and wife and children and brothers and sisters, yes, and even his own life, he cannot be my disciple. Whoever does not bear his own cross and come after me cannot be my disciple" (Lk. 14:26–27, ESV).

Another way to say this is that you will be the very best husband you can be or the very best wife you can be when you love Jesus *more* than your spouse. If you love your spouse second-best, you love him or her in the best possible way.

But if you get this wrong, if you put your husband or your wife or even your hopes in being a husband or wife or father or mother above your love for Christ, you are asking of that human relationship what it is incapable of giving. This is what idols always are. They are finite, created things that we are trying to trick infinite grace out of. We are trying to find in them what God offers to us in Himself. We are immortals, made for infinite joy and glory. And the only place we can find that is in the infinite God Himself.

An idol need not be an actual statue or image. It can just as easily be an image in your head, a scene of happiness, an expectation of the "perfect" husband, the "perfect" wife, the "perfect" sex, the "perfect" children, family, house, job, whatever. That's still a *graven* image; it's still an *imagined* reality that you are placing your hopes in for your joy, happiness, pleasure, or success, but your husband cannot be all that you need. Your wife cannot be all that you need. Marriage and family are truly wonderful gifts of God, but they must be received with gratitude for what they actually are and not for what you wish they would be.

Again, my point here is not to rain on your romance. My point is to help you put your love life in the right place, namely, *below* your love of God. When we order our loves rightly, it frees us to love and be loved more freely, more gladly according to the purposes of God. We want our expectations to be as high as God's are and not any higher (and not any lower). We want to receive from God what He has for us in the gift of marriage. If we take Scripture seriously (as we should), it turns out that marriage is a huge gift, full of blessing. "He who finds a wife finds a good thing, and obtains favor from the LORD" (Prov. 18:22, ESV).

This starting point of finding our ultimate identity in Christ teaches us how to love and value our spouse biblically. There are unique responsibilities given to husbands and wives, and we will get to those soon, but the first thing is to view one another in Christ. In the first instance, you are not "husband and wife"; in the first instance you are brother and sister. God created man in His image: male and female He created them. Man and woman share equally in God's image. Men and women have unique ways of displaying the glory of God, but we were created to rule the world together, to bear God's image together, to be friends, companions, brothers, and sisters. And this fundamental equality in worth, in dignity, in bearing God's image in the world is underlined by our salvation in Christ.

In Christ, there are no distinctions in the grace bestowed to men or women (Gal. 3:28). Just as there is neither Jew nor Greek, slave nor free, "if you are Christ's, then you are Abraham's offspring, heirs according to the promise" (Gal. 3:29, ESV). In fact, this is one of those places where modern Bible translations often mess things up. There's a reason why the Bible freely refers to all Christians as "sons" and "brothers," but many modern Bible translators, out of fear that women might feel left out, adjust the language to the gender neutral "children" or the so-called inclusive "brothers *and sisters*." But Paul knows exactly what he's doing: "But when the fullness of time had come, God sent forth his Son, born of a woman, born under the law, to redeem those who were under the law, so that we might receive adoption *as sons*" (Gal. 4:4–5, ESV, emphasis mine). This is not a remotely sexist thing. We are all sons (men and women alike) because we have been adopted "as sons" in and through the work of God's Son. In the ancient world it was common for an inheritance to be passed down through free male heirs. But the whole point of this passage is actually to affirm the inheritance of those who might be thought to be left out (slaves, Gentiles, women). Paul says that all of them have received the adoption of *sons* in the Son. In other words, to make this point in modern, virtue-signaling parlance, "sons" and "brothers" in Christ are *inclusive* biblical terms, and we do well not to try to improve upon God's own word choices.

Peter makes a very similar point when he says that a husband must honor his wife as a *co-heir* of the grace of life (1 Pet. 3:7). This means that a man should look at his wife or fiancée and gasp. Do you know what God has given you or is in the process of giving you? That woman, that terrifying, glorious woman made in His image, was created by God and redeemed with the precious blood of Jesus and the Holy Spirit has taken up residence in her. She is of immense value to God. She is precious to Him. She is His daughter, an heir of the promise, a co-heir of the grace of life with you. Do you feel that? Does it make your chest knot up? Do you get a little bit afraid? Maybe a lot afraid? Good. Hold that pose.

C.S. Lewis writes,

> It is a serious thing to live in a society of possible gods and goddesses, to remember that the dullest and most uninteresting person you talk to may one day be a creature which, if you saw it now, you would be strongly tempted to worship, or else a horror and a corruption such as you now meet, if at all, only in a nightmare. All day long we are, in some degree, helping each other to one or the other of these destinations. It is in the light of these overwhelm-

ing possibilities, it is with the awe and the circumspection proper to them, that we should conduct all of our dealings with one another, all friendships, all loves, all play, all politics. There are no ordinary people. You have never talked to a mere mortal. Nations, cultures, arts, civilizations—these are mortal, and their life is to ours as the life of a gnat. But it is immortals whom we joke with, work with, marry, snub, and exploit—immortal horrors or everlasting splendors.[1]

So then, there is nothing in all of creation by which you may get closer to the presence of the living God than when you are in the presence of another human being. This is absolutely true, and how much more ought a man to think this of his own wife? How much more ought a woman to think this of her husband? Part of what makes *Christian* marriage such a blessing is the opportunity to share life with another human being made in God's image, cleansed by the blood of Christ, indwelt by the Holy Spirit, destined for everlasting splendor. There are no mere mortals. You are married to an immortal. You will marry an immortal. God's creation of man in His own image is more than enough to inspire deep reverence and awe for all human life, and an even deeper reverence for *redeemed* human life in Christ, but the gift of Christian marriage brings that reverence home.

This is no empty reverence. It is not merely the fact of *future* glory or *future* horror that ought to give us significant pause. It is also the fact that we are building that

---

1. *The Weight of Glory* (New York: Macmillan: 1980), 18–19.

glory or horror right now, this minute. Immortals do no insignificant things. Going to work, going to school, writing, building, singing, laughing, eating—in all of these things we are shaping and being shaped into what we will be forever. And then on top of all of that, we are also entrusted with making new people, more immortals. We are bringing them into existence through biological conception, but the project hardly ends there. All day long, we are in varying degrees helping to form the kind of person who is aiming for everlasting glory or everlasting disgust.

This begins in the marriage covenant itself. We are loving and serving, leading and following, giving and receiving in a way that is either aimed at eternal glory, peace, and joy, or not. But lest this seem all too esoteric, we are also simply talking about whether our marriages line up with Heaven or not. Families are where immortals are made. And this means that the act of forming new families and growing them and maintaining them in a Christian way means recognizing that there is immortality wound through it all. It all has significance and meaning because of eternity. There is no extraneous dirty dish washed, no floor scrubbed, no encouraging word given, no comforting hug extended, no day of hard work offered that goes unnoticed, that gets lost in the cosmos—in Christ, none of it is in vain. We are building a kingdom that cannot be shaken. That kingdom is principally built out of *people*. But many of those people were made out of peanut butter and jelly sandwiches prepared with Christian love. And that love will live forever.

QUESTIONS FOR DISCUSSION

1. On the day after your wedding, what will not have changed?

2. How can people make idols in their imaginations or expectations concerning marriage? Are you tempted to this in any way?

3. How do modern Bible translations sometimes obscure a really important point about men and women in Christ (see Gal. 4:4–5)? Why does it matter?

4. What does C.S. Lewis say about people? What are the two possibilities he highlights?

5. How does the idea of your spouse or fiancé/fiancée being an "immortal" make you think about him/her? How does it shape how you think about marriage/family?

CHAPTER 3

TAKING OUT THE GARBAGE

To center us once again: We began with our identities in Christ because it is the most important thing. It defines us. It makes us who we are and everything else follows from that. What we will be forever is what we are growing into today.

We start with our identities in Christ because it immediately teaches us how to relate to others, and, in this instance, how to relate to our spouse. Sin messes with everything, but one of the most obvious places is in relationships. Sin destroys. Sin disfigures. Sin tears things apart. Sin complicates. Sin distorts. We didn't even need to note that here—if you're reading this book, you already know it. In fact, when you told your testimony, you might have talked about some of the areas where sin has broken things in your life and in your family. Apart from Christ, marriage really seems like the dumbest thing in the world. Why in the world is it a good idea for a sinful, selfish man and a sinful, selfish woman to make promises to love one another with Christian love in front of a bunch of their family and friends? Why would any sane people do this?

In fact, in some ways, our modern cultural aversion to marriage actually has some sanity mixed in with all the confusions. In so far as our culture has turned away from Jesus and the way He made the world, there may be at least a little bit of sanity in the conclusion that marriage is for the birds. Why do that to yourself? Why shoot yourself in the foot? Sinners break stuff. Sinners ruin things. Why bother with all that expensive stuff when chances are good we're going to blow it all up? Unfortunately for our culture, though, as it turns out, marriage is actually quite a bit like gravity. It's woven into the fabric of creation. So even unbelieving pagans are better off embracing marriage and family than not.

But apart from the redeeming grace of God, the unbelieving reluctance surrounding marriage has a point. But what if God really changes sinners? What if, by the grace of God, a man can slowly begin to learn how to love a woman like Christ loves the Church and gave Himself for her? What if, by the grace of God, a woman really can begin to learn how to respect a man, to submit to him as the Church does to Christ? And what if there's blessing for those people and their descendants, by the grace of God, to a thousand generations? What if it's not crazy?

Well, it's not. It's not crazy at all. Okay, well it *is* crazy and it *isn't* crazy all at the same time.

But here's the point: in Christ you have been loved with an everlasting love, and you have been forgiven by the blood of Christ. In Christ, you have been given the resources you need to love others *into eternity*, not least of which includes the man you've agreed to let sleep next to you for the rest of your life. In Christ, you have been given the resources you need to forgive others *into eternity*, not least of which includes the woman you've asked to sleep next to you for the rest of your life.

In Luke 7, a sinful woman shows up and begins anointing the feet of Jesus with her tears and precious oil while He's at dinner with a Pharisee. The Pharisee is fairly sure that this proves that Jesus is not a prophet, but Jesus, knowing the Pharisee's thoughts, replies that this woman has shown Him real love. "Her sins, which are many, are forgiven, for she loved much. But to whom little is forgiven, the same loves little" (Lk. 7:47, NKJV).

In other words, getting married is crazy if all you have to draw on is good intentions and high hopes. Good luck with that. But if you have met Jesus, you have come into an inheritance that is mind-blowing. If there's forgiveness there *for you* for the rest of your life, and if there's love there for you into eternity, then there's forgiveness for her, there's love for him. In your own strength, you do not have what it takes to love a woman the way God intends for you to love her. You do not have what it takes to forgive him the way he will need to be forgiven. But in Christ, you have been forgiven much, and therefore in

Christ, you have the resources, the riches of *His* inheritance sealed to you in the person of the Holy Spirit to love and to forgive *much*.

In fact, Scripture says that love covers a *multitude* of sins (Prov. 10:12, 1 Pet. 4:8).

So let's make this very practical. A Christian is someone who confesses sin, seeks forgiveness, and forgives others *regularly*. This is like doing the dishes or doing your laundry or changing the oil in your truck. This is the basic maintenance of Christian joy. John writes,

> And these things write we unto you, that your joy may be full. This then is the message which we have heard of him, and declare unto you, that God is light, and in him is no darkness at all. If we say that we have fellowship with him, and walk in darkness, we lie, and do not the truth: but if we walk in the light, as he is in the light, we have fellowship with one another, and the blood of Jesus Christ his Son cleanseth us from all sin. If we say that we have no sin, we deceive ourselves, and the truth is not in us. If we confess our sins, he is faithful and just to forgive us our sins, and to cleanse us from all unrighteousnes. (1 Jn. 1:4–9)

If you are a Christian, at your core is the joy of being forgiven. And therefore, you cannot help but become a *forgiver*. Being a Christian doesn't mean that you don't sin. Being a Christian means you know what to do about sin. The difference between a clean house and a messy house on the same street—both with big families and lots of kids—is not that in the clean house they don't make messes. Not hardly. No, the difference between the clean house and the messy house is that in the clean house they *pick up*. They take out the garbage, they do the dishes, they do the laundry. The difference between a clean heart and a messy heart is that in the clean heart, the cleansing blood of Jesus is being regularly applied. A clean heart (in this fallen world) is not a heart that never has any sin; it's a heart where sin is regularly being confessed and forgiven. And notice that this is where Christian *fellowship* comes from. We have fellowship with one another when the blood of Christ *cleanses* us through confession and forgiveness. This is especially important for fellowship in Christian marriage. More on that in a moment.

Parents of toddlers should learn a simple fact fairly early on: toddlers make messes. They spill their milk. They drop glass jars. They pull things off of tables. This is just what toddlers do. It makes no sense at all for a parent to ask a two-year-old how they could have spilled their grape juice on the carpet. That's just what toddlers do. Of course, wise parents begin to take various precautions (yay for sippy cups), but wise parents also need to recognize that they have plenty of resources for cleaning up messes. Many parents make a bigger mess in their homes with their anger and frustration than their toddlers ever do with spaghetti and meatballs. And this is also true of our temptations when dealing with sin. Christians can sin on top of their sin, responding angrily, lying, minimizing, cultivating bitterness, making excuses—when we, of all people, know what to do with sin. We, of all people, know the solution to all sin is the cleansing blood of Jesus.

If we confess our sins, He is faithful and just to forgive us our sins, and to cleanse us from all unrighteousness.

Hopefully, whether you have been married for many years, only a few years, or you are only planning to get married pretty soon, you have already begun to practice this grace in your life and in your relationship together. This doesn't mean that a healthy relationship is constantly fighting and bickering—that's a really bad sign—but if you are ordinary descendants of Adam and Eve, there have been at least a few places where someone said something or failed to say something or forgot about something or showed up late or misunderstood something, and in those moments when someone blew it, hopefully you practiced one of the most basic skills Christians should have. Hopefully you quickly confessed your sins, you forgave one another, and *fellowship* was restored. And when you did that, you were practicing for Heaven. You were living like immortals.

Let me say something more here about *fellowship*. Christians need to understand this notion of fellowship, and they need to understand it down in their bones. Now, there are different spheres of fellowship in the world. It is a Christian duty to be in fellowship with all true and faithful Christians so far as it depends upon us. Sometimes there are real snarls and tangles, and we find ourselves out of fellowship with other Christians, despite our best attempts to make things right. But we should never be in a position where we are withholding fellowship from someone who is repentant. "Then came Peter to him, and said, Lord, how oft shall my brother sin against me, and

I forgive him? till seven times? Jesus saith unto him, I say not unto thee, Until seven times: but, Until seventy times seven" (Matt. 18:21–22). Well, that's pretty clear, isn't it? How many times do you have to forgive? How many times do you have to restore fellowship? *You can't count that high.* And remember that standard is God's standard with you. He is committed to forgiving and receiving you way beyond seventy times seven times.

At the same time, what Jesus is saying here about forgiveness and fellowship does not necessitate *trust* in every direction. A painter from your church may do a shoddy job on your basement, and he may admit this and ask your forgiveness, and you should forgive him completely, and you still might not call him for your next painting need. Your heart should be in a good place such that you can happily worship next to him the following Lord's Day, but fellowship and forgiveness don't mean that you think he's the greatest painter ever. Same thing applies to all sorts of vocations and skills. And this is why you might be in perfectly good Christian fellowship with a brother in the Lord and not trust him at all to be your husband. That's a perfectly reasonable conclusion in many cases and need not be uncharitable in the slightest. The standards for marriage are higher than the standards for being in fellowship. Likewise, when there has been an egregious breach of the marriage covenant (e.g., adultery), forgiveness must always be extended, but the future of the marriage depends on restoring trust (more on that in a later chapter).

Next, apply this principle to your spouse or soon-to-be spouse. How many times shall your husband sin against you and you forgive him? Seven times? Jesus says, no, ma'am, you can't count that high. And obviously, the fellowship requirement for marriage goes even deeper than the fellow who painted the basement, but the principles really are the same. If you've married a godly man or woman, they have opinions and perspectives and convictions on any number of subjects. God has ordained an order to the marriage relationship that we will get to in more detail in a bit, but the short version is that a woman agrees to submit to her husband in the Lord, and that means that she agrees to give her opinions and input, and then to follow his lead. This doesn't necessitate that a wife always immediately and in every detail *agree* with her husband. But her marriage vows *do* mean that she is enthusiastically on his team—that's the fellowship part. Nevertheless, this is where one of those "preparing for marriage" checklists can be really handy. Hopefully, you've already managed to talk through lots of different topics: theology, worship, finances, politics, entertainment standards, marital roles, children, education, health and nutritional standards, etc. And a wise woman will have a great deal of input for her husband and sometimes not share his exact perspective. But when she says, "I do," she is promising to follow that man in the Lord, submitting to him in everything, to be on his team, and to be in fellowship with him.

There's an enormous difference between having different perspectives or opinions on some subject and being out of fellowship. Being out of fellowship means you have lost your temper. It means you have sinned against one another. It means you have a grudge, or you are bitter, or you have resentment. A Christian may have all kinds of patience and grace for working through different perspectives, but a Christian should have no patience for sin. Jesus is clear: "Therefore if thou bring thy gift to the altar, and there rememberest that thy brother hath ought against thee; leave there thy gift before the altar, and go thy way; first be reconciled to thy brother, and then come and offer thy gift" (Matt. 5:23–24). Jesus says that being in fellowship is a prerequisite for worship. Paul argues similarly regarding the Lord's Supper in Corinth. The Corinthians were grabbing and hogging and getting drunk, and Paul said that because of their divisions, they were not actually celebrating the Lord's Supper (1 Cor. 11:18–21). Elsewhere, Paul writes: "Be ye angry, and sin not: let not the sun go down upon your wrath: neither give place to the devil" (Eph. 4:26–27).

So Christians must be watchful and persistent in this. Hebrews says that bitterness is a root that springs up and brings trouble with it, defiling many (12:15). You do not want that trouble in your home, in your marriage, in your life. So be quick to confess your sins and quick to forgive from the heart. As Pastor Douglas Wilson likes to say, "Keep short accounts." Don't let a backlog of sins build up. Love keeps no record of wrongs (1 Cor. 13:5). Love deals with sin right away. And since the devil likes to get a foothold here, let me just point out that sometimes marital bumps will occur at the most inopportune moments, e.g., on the way to church, just as friends are walking up to your house for dinner (maybe even *during* a dinner party), or late at night when everyone is tired and not thinking clearly. Make it a point to deal with sin right away. Do not walk into church out of fellowship. Leave your gift at the altar. Be five minutes late and be reconciled first. Welcome your dinner guests inside and briefly excuse yourselves in order to get back into fellowship quickly. If you're at a crowded party and something pops, lean over and whisper your confession and forgiveness. One of the wonderful gifts of cell phones and texting and email is our ability to make things right quickly that way, too.

A couple of miscellaneous notes on all of this. First, endeavor to use biblical language for your sin. Do not call your lie "fudging details" or your anger "an emotional response." Related, don't just say "sorry" or "my bad." Actually state your sin, that it was wrong because God says so, and say the words, "Will you forgive me?"

Second, if you're on the receiving end of an apology, don't be picky about the exact words, and when you say, "I forgive you," consider your forgiveness as a promise to not hold the sin against them. In that moment the sin might still sting a bit and, depending on the offense, it really may take some time to heal, but you need not and should not withhold forgiveness until you *feel* forgiving. That's a great way to not actually heal or ever *feel* forgiving. Forgiveness is a promise, not a feeling. You have been forgiven freely by God, so freely forgive, and let God take care of the healing part. If you're not in the habit of confessing sin and forgiving quickly, some of this might seem awkward in the beginning, but like many good things, you can actually become good at it. It's always a bit embarrassing, but it's always an opportunity to glory in the cross. We are Christians, and confession of sin and forgiveness are central to our Christian joy. Christian marriages and homes are not clean because we don't make messes; they are clean because we've learned to pick up. We have fellowship with one another because the blood of Jesus washes us clean.

Also, remember that love *covers* a multitude of sins. When we explicitly confess our sins and forgive one another, we are dealing with sin like Christians, and that is love in action too. But part of the glory of the gospel is God's commitment *not* to mark every sin. "If thou, LORD, shouldest mark iniquities, O Lord, who shall stand? But there is forgiveness with thee, that thou mayest be feared" (Ps. 130:3–4). The wonderful promise of 1 John 1:9 includes the fact that while we are required to confess the sins we know about, God promises to cleanse us from *all* unrighteousness. It's astounding. We're like little kids come in from playing in the mud, covered head to toe in grime, and we hold up our hands and ask our Dad if he can wash our *hands*. And He smiles and laughs and says, *Yes, of course, I will wash you completely clean.* And if that's how God our Father is with us, that's how we must be with one another, with our spouses and children. Quick to forgive, quick to overlook little sins, quick to cover sin with love. But if you are covering sin in love, then you really must cover it in love. You cannot decide three weeks later to bring it up after all—that's bitterness. That's keeping a record of wrongs. If you cover an offense in love, let it go completely, freely, gladly, just like so many of your sins have been covered in love by your heavenly Father.

Of course, some sins need to be addressed and confronted, and should not be simply covered in love. Nevertheless, you must not be that unforgiving servant who was forgiven millions of dollars and then went out and started strangling his fellow servant for five bucks. Do not receive the forgiveness of Christ and then harbor a bad attitude about your husband leaving his socks on the floor or the way your wife organizes the pantry.

Lastly, don't miss the fact that this commitment—to confession of sin and seventy-times-seven forgiveness and covering crowds of sins in love and staying in fellowship—is built on the foundation of our shared fellowship in Christ. Of course, we are to show this same kind of love and grace to unbelievers, but as brothers and sisters in the Lord, the watching world will know that we know Jesus by our love for one another. And when we practice this grace, we are practicing the grace of eternal life. We are pressing one another on toward Christ and His glorious immortality.

QUESTIONS FOR DISCUSSION

1. *What's crazy about getting married? Should unbelievers get married?*

2. *Why is it not crazy for Christians to get married?*

3. *How do Christian hearts and homes stay "clean"?*

4. *What's the difference between being in fellowship and having different opinions or perspectives?*

5. *What is forgiveness? How should our feelings be involved?*

CHAPTER 4

COVENANT ASYMMETRY

HAVING established that there is a wonderful and glorious dignity found in being created in the image of God, and, furthermore, a wonderful and glorious equality found in our inheritance in the gospel—that we are immortals who will grow into Christ-like glory together for all of eternity, we turn to the differences between men and women, male and female, and in particular, the different roles God gives to a husband and wife. But as we do so, do not lose sight of the main point: these differences are still aimed at that eternal glory; they are not merely decorations for that immortality, they are actually essential components for growing into that glory.

So, to begin with, I would like to break several laws in various states and countries by stating simply: men and women are different.

G.K. Chesterton says in his poem *Comparisons* that people are the kind of fools that, as soon as someone starts describing the differing glories of the sun and the moon, a minute later will start claiming that one is better than the other. But difference does not imply lesser value. This is like claiming that hammers are better than tea cups, or earrings are better than screwdrivers. The fact that things are different is a gift and an opportunity, and only a fool would think that one thing is best for everything. Everything depends on what it is that you are trying to do. Men and women are different kinds of people that are good at many things in common and also have distinguishing gifts and abilities. Women, for example, are the kinds of human beings that can make other human beings *inside of themselves*. And men are the kinds of human beings that think it is fun to launch other men into outer space. And obviously, one of those is *way* cooler.

Heh, that's a joke, people.

So the Bible teaches that there is a wonderful and foundational equality that men and women share in the image of God and redemption, and at the same time, there is an asymmetry or inequality to their respective glories. And this is wonderful. God made both men and women in His image, but that image of God is not manifested in the exact same ways in male and female—the image of God is not revealed in the exact same *shape*. And this is part of what God created and saw and declared *very good* (Gen. 1:31). And therefore, we should agree with God. It's not just kind of good, it's very good.

"But I would have you know, that the head of every man is Christ; and the head of the woman is the man; and the head of Christ is God ... he is the image and glory of God: but the woman is the glory of the man" (1 Cor. 11:3, 7). Paul goes on to explain that both men and women need each other and are not independent of one another, but nevertheless this natural order and the respective, mutually-dependent glories are displayed even in how nature teaches men and women to wear their hair differently (1 Cor. 11:14–15). Likewise, this creational asymmetry has implications for the Church. Paul writes, "But I suffer not a woman to teach, nor to usurp authority over the man, but to be in silence. For Adam was first formed, then Eve. And Adam was not deceived, but the woman being deceived was in the transgression" (1 Tim. 2:12–14). In these places and elsewhere, Scripture makes it clear that there are natural and God-ordained differences between men and women.

We will unpack this asymmetry more as we go along, but needless to say, we live in a world that is terribly confused about what it means to be a man or a woman. This is driven by a fundamental hatred of the One whose image they bear, but it is impossible for the hatred of the Maker to be disconnected from all that He has made. And it turns out that hierarchy, asymmetry, difference, and inequality are wound through the entire created order. Not only is God the head of Christ and man the head of woman, so too this same order and hierarchy can be seen in the celestial bodies, the animal kingdom, plants, and even inanimate minerals and substances.

Now you may have noticed that I used the word "inequality," and you might think I should take that back. But this is directly related to what I mean by "asymmetry." Qualitative differences are not only the basis for all the wonderful variations of taste and texture and beauty we enjoy, but they are also the basis for all progress. The fact that God made things *different* is what gives them their distinctive strengths, weaknesses, uses, purposes— and *glory*. The fact that certain foods provide certain vitamins and health benefits is their *glory*. The fact that certain metals or minerals are harder or softer gives them different uses. At the center of all of it is the fundamental difference between the sexes. The irony of our modern egalitarian overlords is that their proposed path to progress is absolute and universal equality. But absolute, universal equality (equality in *every way*) is a world of complete monotony. Universal equality is universal uniformity and repetition. A world without qualitative difference is a boring and tedious oblivion. It is quite literally Ichabod— the glory has departed. Striving for equality in every direction, in every way is a certain path to utter stagnation and regression. If all you have are hammers in the tool box, no matter how useful hammers are for certain purposes, they do not have the same strengths and abilities as jigsaws or screwdrivers or nails. Ditto for having the same materials, same personalities, and same exact gifts. What a great way to *not* get things done. What a great way to *not* be able to create, invent, or improve upon things.

If we are to be Christians in our thinking, we must begin with a robust celebration of creational difference and hierarchy, expecting to find glories and opportunities and true progress as we come to understand what the differences are *for*. All creational differences line up in some way with the way God made the world. These sexual differences are not random or capricious but sexual *assignments*. And God does not give assignments that are worthless or accidental. And these assignments are not merely temporary, they are eternal. Our masculinity and femininity are assignments that begin here but will grow in glory forever. Our sexual differences will not diminish or fade but will sharpen and glisten with ever increasing majesty.

So we need to return to Scripture in humility and submission, receiving our assignments of being created male or female with faith and joy. There's a great deal to this that could fill many books, but for those of you who are preparing to take vows and move in with your new spouse shortly, you really should read the fine print for the assignments that are specific to marriage. Do you know what you are signing up for? This goes all the more for those of you who are already married—even if you have been for years! Yes, I know you're in love, but have you reviewed what God actually requires of you? Are you ready to obey? There is great freedom in obedience, submitting to what God has made you for.

So what does the fine print actually say?

Paul begins his exhortations on marriage in Ephesians 5 by speaking to the wives first. So let's talk about wives first. It says, "Wives, submit to your own husbands, as unto the Lord ... Therefore as the church is subject unto Christ, so let the wives be to their own husbands in every thing" (Eph. 5:22, 24). When I was engaged to my wife, I remember talking to her on the phone one time after having read something with her about marriage, and she stopped me and asked, "Now, when it says *submit*, it doesn't really mean *submit*, does it?" And I hemmed and hawed my way through a sort of, kind of, affirmative answer. And friends, the fact that we have now celebrated twenty years of a really joyful marriage is an example of God's *grace*.

Yes, the word means *submit* (even in Greek: I checked). But we live in a world in high rebellion against God and against His word, such that even many *Christians* are busy trying to dig God out of the hole they think He dug for Himself. So, many Christians will say, "Well, wait a second, if you read the previous verse, you'll see that Paul just exhorted *all* Christians to submit to one another (Eph. 5:21). See there? Paul's just reminding wives of that general exhortation." Um, actually he's not.

Yes, there is a general and mutual submission in the Lord for all Christians. We covered that in the first few chapters. Yes, there is a mutual submission in the Lord as brother or sister in Christ, as co-heirs of the grace of life, as fellow disciples of Jesus. That's the mutual reverence and deference you share for one another as *no mere mortals*. Yes, got that. But that's *not* what Paul is talking about in the next verse. It is certainly true that general reverence for Christ and for one another drives and undergirds the following commands, but Paul is not merely reiterating that general exhortation, otherwise his command to husbands makes no sense. Let me state it clearly: The Bible *does* teach a mutual submission insofar as the man and the woman are both human beings made in the image of God and Christians and co-heirs of the grace of life. But the Bible does *not* teach mutual submission when it comes to the *roles* of husband and wife. The husband does not and must not submit to his wife with respect to his duties as a husband. This is because the wife "should submit in every thing" to her husband (Eph. 5:24). After she submits in everything to her husband, what is there left for her husband to submit to his wife in?

The closest thing to a legitimate response to that question is what Paul says about sex:

> The husband should give to his wife her conjugal rights, and likewise the wife to her husband. For the wife does not have authority over her own body, but the husband does. Likewise the husband does not have authority over his own body, but the wife does. Do not deprive one another, except perhaps by agreement for a limited time, that you may devote yourselves to prayer; but then come together again, so that Satan may not tempt you because of your lack of self-control. (1 Cor. 7:3–5, ESV)

There is a clear mutuality in the marriage bed, but this mutuality actually inverts the egalitarianism of our day and in no way supports it. Christian mutuality surrenders the self to the other, rather than demanding rights for the self. So when a Christian woman says, "I do," she is surrendering her body to her husband, and a Christian man is surrendering his body to his wife when he says the same. We should note that this means that the woman has true authority in the marriage. To submit to her husband "in every thing" does not mean she has no authority. We know this because clearly she has authority over her husband's body. And yet, even this mutual authority in the marriage bed in no way sets aside the husband's general authority over his wife. He is responsible before God and therefore has authority from God to teach his wife to rule his body faithfully.

And here is perhaps the clearest example of the goodness and productivity of hierarchy and submission to God's sexual assignments. The woman has certain sexual powers, and the man has certain sexual powers. And in the act of sexual intercourse, the woman submits to and receives from the man who loves and gives himself. And this is how the most valuable resource in the whole universe comes into being: new people. *Immortal* people.

Part of the problem we have when talking about submission and headship is that we've completely lost the biblical categories that accompany thinking *covenantally*. After Babel, when God determined to fulfill His mission to save the world, He made a *covenant* with Abraham (Gen. 15:18). Inherent in that covenant were notions of representation and responsibility, submission and authority. God made His covenant with Abram, but it also explicitly included his entire household: his wife, future generations of children, even his servants (Gen. 15, 17:22–27)—the people Abram was responsible for, people who submitted to Abram's authority.

In other words, when God made covenant with Abram, God recognized Abram as the "head" of his household. The Old Testament sign of the covenant was circumcision, so all the males of his house were circumcised. They all *submitted* to the covenant headship of Abram. They identified with him. But of course most importantly, by identifying with Abram, they were identifying with Yahweh, the God of Abram. Just as Abram believed God and that was accounted to him as righteousness (Gen. 15:6), the covenant was a standing invitation to the household of Abram to trust in God with him and so receive that same righteous standing before God. All of this is finally fulfilled in Jesus: "Now to Abraham and his seed were the promises made. He saith not, and to seeds, as of many; but as of one, and to thy seed, which is Christ ... And if ye be Christ's, then are ye Abraham's seed, and heirs according to the promise" (Gal. 3:16, 29).

Paul reasons the same way in Ephesians 5. "For the husband is the head of the wife even as Christ is the head of the church, his body, and is himself its Savior. Now as the church submits to Christ, so also wives should submit in everything to their husbands" (verses 23–24, ESV). More on headship in a minute, but for now understand that submission in marriage means standing in the place of the Church with regard to Christ. This is not a position of scorn or disgrace; it is a position of true glory. And again, we see the means by which God has determined to fill the earth with fruitfulness. It is the efficacious love of Christ for His Bride, the Church, that is progressively filling this world with life and love and peace and joy. The fruit of the Spirit isn't just some ethereal qualities; it is good for science, business, economics, politics, and foreign affairs. The fruit of the Spirit truly makes the world a better place.

One of the ways I like to unpack what this submission and headship mean is by asking: What does a Christian woman's submission to her husband *not* mean? Some of this we have already answered implicitly. Wifely submission does not mean being a man's property or second-rate humans, or much less, second-class citizens of the Kingdom of God. A Christian woman's submission does not mean she has nothing to say or even that she does not have strong opinions or input for her husband. Actually, the woman was created to be Adam's *helper* (Gen. 2:20). As some misguided feminists and egalitarians like to point out (for misguided reasons), this is the same word used in other places to describe God's own ministry to people in various ways (e.g., Gen. 49:25, Exod. 18:4). God is our Helper. The Holy Spirit is our *Helper*, our Comforter, our Advocate (Jn. 14:16, 26, 15:26, Rom. 8:26). This is all true and underlines the enormous dignity and glory of being a Christian wife, and it in no way excuses exegetical gymnastics that attempt to explain away a Christian wife's abiding duty to give that help and assistance *in submission* to her husband (unlike the Holy Spirit). Nevertheless, a man should want and welcome his wife's input and opinions and concerns, even when they differ from his, and this should not be seen as in any way inconsistent with her duty to submit to him in all things.

One of the ways the Holy Spirit comforts our hearts is through the book of Psalms. In fact, Paul says that we are to be filled with the Spirit by singing Psalms (Eph. 5:18–19). The Church submits to Christ in part by praying and singing the Psalms back to Him. And so this is one of the ways we can learn about what it means for a wife to submit to her husband in everything. How is the bride of Christ instructed to speak to her husband, Christ? The book of Psalms is an inspired script of possible options. What we find in the Psalms are many prayers of praise, respect, honor, remembering God's greatness and salvation. Therefore, a wife should work hard to praise her husband, speak highly to him and about him, and thank him for his faithfulness, loyalty, hard work, paying the bills, and so on. This is what respect and honor *do*. Just as praise and thanksgiving fill the psalms, praise and thanksgiving should be on a wife's lips regularly. Nevertheless, we also find Psalms of lament and sadness, one of which says something like, "Where have you been all day? Why have you not answered any of my texts? I'm surrounded by people in diapers. Will you not come speedily with chocolate ice cream and deliver me?" (Trust me, it's in the Hebrew.) Of course, there are ways for a wife to spout a lament or complaint that are sinful and disrespectful, just like it's possible to sin while praying to God with a really crummy attitude. But the point here is simply that just as the Church cries out to God in suffering and pain, just as the Church pours out her heart to her Lord, so too it is not unsubmissive for a Christian wife to pour out her heart to her husband. In fact, that is what a healthy marriage looks like.

In the book of Proverbs, wisdom is a woman. The young man is being taught by his parents to recognize her voice crying out, to seek her out, doing everything to find her, and to marry her. A wise Christian man understands that a godly Christian wife is one of the central ways God is granting him *wisdom*. A man who does not have this conviction should be avoided like the plague, no matter how big his bank account or how fast his cars or how large his theological library (perhaps *especially* if he has a large theological library). At the same time, a wife should labor to make her input truly *helpful*, respectful, and useful. And while a wise man routinely implements the input of his wife, a wise woman should not be offended when he does not.

There is another important detail in the fine print, which is the phrase "*your own* husband" (Eph. 5:22). Christianity does not teach that all women everywhere must submit to all men everywhere. It is true that women are the glory of man (everywhere and in every place), and it is shameful for men to attempt to be the glory of man (or the glory of women) through various forms of softness and effeminacy. There are creational differences and distinctions that run all the way through the created order and should be honored everywhere, as historically designated by cultural practices such as standing when a woman enters the room, waiting for a hostess to begin eating, curtseying and bowing, etc. But the particular assignment of submission given to a Christian wife is unique to marriage.

However, there are other analogous assignments of submission, such as the submission that Christians owe their elders (Heb. 13:17) and the submission Christians owe civil authorities (1 Pet. 2:13). Speaking of which, people don't generally freak out when we quote a Bible verse in favor of submitting to police officers. Is that tyrannical, denigrating, oppressive, or dehumanizing to the non-police officers among us? Political authority can certainly be abused, and no human authority is absolute, but this merely exposes our modern idolatries and prejudices. We give political authorities a far greater pass because modern secularism (falsely) believes that the state is the savior of the family and the Church. The Enlightenment proclaimed that all our wars and woes came from tribalism and religious zeal, and it lifted up the Most Holy State as the secular gospel of hope for the family and the Church. And this ushered in the twentieth century, almost certainly the bloodiest century this world has ever seen between all the wars and genocides, including abortion. But please don't bother us with the facts, sir.

Ah, where was I? Oh right, a wife's submission to her *own* husband—when a Christian woman promises to submit to her own husband, she is not promising to submit to all men everywhere. Related to this principle is the fact that Christians do not believe in arranged marriages. I would not go so far as to say it is always sinful, but I would argue that it is sub-biblical. Even in Genesis, where the family was heavily involved in the marriage arrangements for Isaac and Rebekah, the choice is still clearly given to Rebekah whether she would be Isaac's wife or not (Gen. 24). Thus, in every Christian marriage ceremony, the woman takes vows alongside the man. This is very important for a number of reasons, but one of them is to underline the fact that a Christian woman chooses to marry one man freely of her own volition. No Christian woman is forced to marry any man. A Christian woman has the dignity and honor of saying "no" to any man she pleases. She would do well to seek out godly counsel and wisdom in her decision-making, particularly from her parents and pastors, but when she decides to say, "I do," she is a free Christian woman making her own choice. And this choice includes the decision to enter into *Christian* marriage, which means she is choosing to submit herself to this one man in everything. Feminists are all about feminine *choice* unless it contradicts what they have decided every woman must choose. So much for feminine freedom.

This free choice to submit to this one man in marriage—when it is done in obedience to God—is a gloriously freeing decision for a woman. When received in faith, the gift of a husband gives enormous orientation to a woman. She signs up to help *this* man, to be devoted to *this* man, to find her gifts and strengths oriented to *this* man. While modernism spreads the lie that infinite possibilities is freedom, anyone who has thought about this for more than half a minute ought to realize that infinite possibilities for finite people is actually a paralyzing slavery.

Biblical limits, God-ordained constraints, set us free to be who we were made to be. So too, when a woman has prayerfully considered a godly man's offer of marriage and consents to that offer, she is agreeing to submit to this man, and there is great freedom in that choice. And that freedom is the path toward becoming what who you really are in Christ, a unique reflection of everlasting splendor.

QUESTIONS FOR DISCUSSION

1. *Why should Christians celebrate hierarchy and difference in general?*

2. *What does a wife's submission to her husband not mean?*

3. *What do the Psalms teach us about a woman's submission to her husband?*

4. *Do women submit to all men in general? What are ways the differences between men and women are still honored in our culture?*

5. *What's the difference between how Christians generally speak about our duty to submit to civil authorities and a wife's submission to her husband? How does that reveal our allegiances or idols?*

CHAPTER 5

SUBMISSION IN THE LORD

" In the Lord" is one of the most important phrases regarding submission and obedience to authorities in Scripture. It shows up in Ephesians 5 in the passage about wives submitting to husbands, which is the focus of this chapter, but it also shows up for children obeying parents (Eph. 6:1), servants with their masters (Eph. 6:5), and elsewhere for submission to civil authorities (1 Pet. 2:13). We will touch on this pattern more later on, but for now, a woman called to submit to her own husband should picture Jesus standing behind her man. Therefore, submission to a husband "in the Lord" is one of the ways a wife pursues Christ, follows Christ, and grows more and more into the likeness of Christ. Understood rightly, submission "in the Lord" is an invitation to an eternal weight of glory.

At the same time, the phrase "in the Lord" is also a wonderfully *limiting* phrase. A husband's authority is not infinite or absolute. In fact, no earthly, human authority is infinite or absolute. All authority on earth is given by God. Therefore, all lawful authority is *derivative* authority. All true, lawful authority in this world is *delegated* authority. A husband has *true* authority over his wife, but it is a *limited* authority. His authority is limited by *his* Lord. Another way to put it is that a man only rightly exercises his authority in his marriage and home when he is *under* the authority of Christ. A man rules well when he is ruled well by Christ. And the same thing goes for police officers, Supreme Court justices, CEOs, and pastors.

Put practically, we can break the world up into basically three categories of decisions or areas where a man may exercise leadership with his wife. The first and the easiest is where a man leads his wife to obey the explicit commands of God found in Scripture. When a man leads his wife to go to church, to pray, to tithe, to practice hospitality, to confess sins and extend forgiveness, he is leading *in the Lord* precisely because he is leading his wife to *obey* what the Lord has explicitly already commanded. It is entirely possible for a man to be a knucklehead while quoting Bible verses. He can insist on going to church like a tyrant, and that really is sinful and wrong, but the fact of his insistence on going to church is a good thing. He might insist on going to a *bad* a church, but that's a somewhat different matter (and we'll come back to that in a moment). When a man leads his wife to obey Christ, this is a great blessing, and a Christian woman should gladly submit to her husband. She should see Christ standing behind her husband, and as he is leading her in obedience to Christ, she should gladly obey.

The second area where a man exercises true authority, and a Christian woman may gladly submit to his leadership, is in those areas of what we may call Christian freedom and Christian wisdom. Where Christ gives us freedom, we have true freedom to use our gifts, resources, and opportunities wisely to the glory of God. The Lord has not forbidden chocolate ice cream on Thursday night or vacationing in the Caribbean in July or hunting elk in October or bright orange sweatshirts or Chinese food or pursuing a sales position in Des Moines. In Christ, we have freedom to pursue and enjoy all good things within the parameters of God's law with joy and thanksgiving. It's still possible for a man to be foolish or to sin in or with any of those things with his attitudes or words or through recklessness or neglect of other duties, but none of those things (or things like them) are sinful in themselves. Christian men have freedom to enjoy various hobbies, pursue various vocations and pastimes, and even have preferences and favorites, and as we discussed in the last chapter, a Christian woman is agreeing to submit to this leadership when she marries a particular man.

Here we can see some of the asymmetry I was talking about earlier. On the one hand, a man asks a woman to marry him because he knows he needs help and because he values the opinions and gifts and glory that she has been given. He knows he needs her wisdom. That is wonderfully true. At the same time, he is asking her to join *him*, and it really isn't the other way around. God created Eve to help Adam, and the order was not random or capricious. The order was on purpose and holds that purpose even today (1 Tim. 2:13). "For the man is not of the woman; but the woman of the man. Neither was the man created for the woman; but the woman for the man" (1 Cor. 11:8–9).

When a couple gets engaged, the woman is not asking him to join her, no matter what they do in the movies and sitcoms. Nor is he asking her to form some sort of cooperative alliance, a mutually-beneficial business contract with 50 percent ownership for each party. No, the woman is agreeing to join this man's mission. This does not obliterate her interests or hobbies or gifts, but in God's ordering, those interests, gifts, and hobbies are oriented toward her husband's mission and not the other way around. And this means if her husband really likes hunting or Caribbean cruises or Mexican food or working for a company in Des Moines or the color orange, in so far as those things are not causing sin, a Christian wife should lean into those interests and preferences enthusiastically. She should submit herself joyfully to him in those lawful areas of Christian freedom.

Once again, a Christian woman should imagine Jesus standing behind her husband in these areas of Christian freedom and wisdom, and this should be an enormous comfort to her as she submits to her husband's decisions about family vacations or financial management or even taking the job offer in Des Moines. A Christian woman should give all the wise counsel and input she can, but she also promises to trust Jesus in giving this particular man to her as her husband. And it should be pointed out once more that when a Christian woman takes her wedding vows, no one is making her do it. She is a free Christian woman, and she is free to say *no* to any man she wants to. And since she is free, she is also free to say yes, if she wants to. But she should be clear in her own mind that what she is saying yes to is *this* particular man, a sinful and fallen man to be sure, but nevertheless, in Christ, a redeemed man, an immortal man with gifts and interests that she is agreeing to be into, to lean into, to submit to, to follow *in the Lord*.

It may seem petty (and it likely *would* be), but better to call the wedding off if his strong preference for the color orange is going to drive you crazy and cause you to sin with a constant bad attitude or critical spirit. But if you are convinced that God has brought this man to you, and you trust God in *that*, then you may also trust Him in all that this may mean down the road. When your husband's judgment leads him to lead you in areas of Christian freedom or wisdom or the color orange, you may continue trusting God *even then*. In fact, it is not really Christian for a woman to place her fundamental trust *in* her husband. No, she trusts her husband precisely because she trusts Jesus *more*. And it is precisely in this give and take of life, the giving of input and advice, the receiving of instruction and decisions, even mixed with the unforeseen hard providences or mistaken judgments, all of it is part of how God is working all things together into an eternal good, for those who love Him and are called according to His purpose (Rom. 8:28). When a woman says "yes" to a particular man, she is also saying "yes" to being shaped by God into a more Christ-like woman through the interests, preferences, gifts, leadership, and love of that particular man.

And this leads to the third category of potential leadership, which is when a husband, even a Christian husband, asks his wife to sin. And here "in the Lord" means that a Christian wife must *not* submit to him. It is not *Christian submission* for a Christian woman to obey her husband when he asks her to look at porn with him. It is actually *Christian* submission in this moment to confront and withstand her husband in his sin. This is Christian love. Now this last category may seem a little on the extremist side of things, but consider this section like the safety talk on the airplane before takeoff. In the unlikely event of a water landing, you really should want to know where the life vests and exits are. You hope your kids never need to exit the house during a fire, but you should occasionally tell them what to do if there is a fire. You hope your wife never needs to defend herself from a home intruder, but you should occasionally remind her where the guns are and make sure she knows how to use them. In a similar way, one of the ways a man protects his wife is by making sure she knows what to do in the event *he* goes off the rails. A wife does not need her husband's permission to obey God rather than him, but it sure makes it easier if he explicitly gives that permission. A husband should tell his wife that if he goes off the rails and starts sinning and refuses to repent, or if he begins leading her in an explicitly sinful direction, she should refuse him and call the elders of the church (or the cops if necessary). And this same principle holds in every area of authority and submission. If civil magistrates or church authorities are going off the rails, citizens and church members should resist and appeal to other appropriate authorities for assistance.

There are numerous ways this sort of disobedience can emerge, but three of the big categories are sexual sin, financial sin, and theological sin. I've already mentioned using pornography above, but of course sexual sin could include any number of things, and in our current cultural climate, any pastor's attempt to list all the possibilities is pretty futile. Nevertheless, we should say that the Christian marriage bed is to be honored: "Marriage is honourable in all, and the bed undefiled: but whoremongers and adulterers God will judge" (Heb. 13:4). This means that a man must be completely faithful to his wife, and discipline all wandering thoughts and eyes. This also means among other things that you should not be getting your sexual goals or advice from *Glamour* magazine or *Playboy* or Triple X dot com. The Song of Songs is inspired Scripture and gives every married couple more to consider than one lifetime of faithful lovemaking will exhaust. But a Christian wife must be both faithful in her submission to her husband's pursuit of her sexually, and she must be faithful not to be led into sexual sin by her husband. More on faithfulness in the marriage bed later.

Occasionally men fall into financial sin, and a Christian wife must not allow her husband to lead her or his family into financial ruin. Skipping ahead a few verses in Ephesians 5, Paul says, "For no man ever yet hated his own flesh; but nourisheth and cherisheth it, even as the Lord the church" (v. 29). Those words *nourish* and *cherish* literally mean to feed and keep warm. This means that a man has a moral responsibility before God to make sure that his wife has a roof over her head, the heating bill paid, sufficient clothing, and food in the pantry. Paul appears to be echoing the law where God limited the practice of polygamy in Israel by requiring that a man not diminish his wife's food, clothing, or sexual rights if he took a second wife (Exod. 21:10). Therefore, it is marital unfaithfulness not to provide these bare minimums. "But if any provide not for his own, and specially for those of his own house, he hath denied the faith, and is worse than an infidel" (1 Tim. 5:8). It may not be a high-handed sin to buy one scratch ticket one time (but why on earth would you?), but a gambling habit, credit card folly, a really foolish business deal, or out of control, compulsive spending really must be confronted by a faithful Christian wife.

It is not unsubmissive to appeal to the elders of the church for input and guidance when you cannot pay the bills or buy food or clothing because your husband lost half his month's salary on a fantasy football bet. At the same time, a man is free to spend his money on vacations and jet skis and hunting rifles, provided he is not failing to honor God through tithing or providing for his household. And he is even free to make foolish choices, provided he is not requiring his wife to break God's law or failing to provide for his family's basic necessities. In other words, if a man is not obeying God's Word, the Christian instinct of his wife should still be to submit to him, in order to win him over to obedience (1 Pet. 3:1). On the other hand, a man is not bound by an extravagant woman's whims or lusts to buy all of the latest fashions every month. "Owe no man any thing, but to love one another; for he that loveth another hath fulfilled the law" (Rom. 13:8). In all of this, a man should be modeling sacrificial generosity and provision, not being stingy or reckless: "Husbands, love your wives, even as Christ loved the church, and gave himself for it" (Eph. 5:25).

Finally, a Christian woman is responsible to be a faithful disciple of Christ while following her husband's spiritual lead. But this doesn't necessitate following your husband absolutely anywhere *spiritually*. There are spiritual wastelands and tar pits that Christian women are responsible before God to avoid. You are required to follow your husband *toward Christ*. And you must not follow him away from Christ. This means that if you married a robust evangelical Protestant man, you should expect him to lead you further into that biblical and theological tradition. But a left turn into Roman Catholicism or Eastern Orthodoxy is not a path toward greater faithfulness, and a complete conversion to either of those heretical branches of the Christian Church would require you to disobey the plain teaching of Scripture. While Peter exhorts wives to win over disobedient husbands without a word by godly conduct (1 Pet. 3:1, and more on that later), that doesn't mean that you must start praying to Mary or St. Bartholomew or kissing icons.

A Christian woman must not pray toward or *through* icons or statues, even if her husband asks her to. A Christian woman must not pray to anyone but the Father, through Jesus His only Son, in the power of the Spirit (Eph. 2:18). A Christian woman must not pray *through* any other mediator than Jesus Christ—He is the only mediator between God and man (1 Tim. 2:5). Nor may a Christian woman go along with any theology that muddles the clear biblical distinctions between justification and sanctification. Justification is by faith alone plus nothing (Gal. 2:16), resulting in the confidence of faith that declares with Paul, "Who shall separate us from the love of Christ? shall tribulation, or distress, or persecution, or famine, or nakedness, or peril, or sword?" (Rom. 8:35). One time I read this verse and the verses following to a woman considering converting to Eastern Orthodoxy, and her reply was that Paul sounded very presumptuous to her. Yes, it's absolutely scandalous for sinful people to talk this way, and yet this is precisely the kind of confidence that justification by faith alone provides. Sanctification is the inevitable result of justification that includes the fruit of the Spirit working out this salvation with fear and trembling and joy. A Christian woman must know her own salvation with this kind of theological clarity and be utterly unmoved by a disobedient husband's wavering on this matter. A woman committed to respecting her husband and seeking to win him back to faithfulness may need to be creative in how she continues to honor her husband, and should seek the biblical counsel of godly elders, but biblical submission means that she resists his disobedient leadership.

A godly woman must refuse to follow her husband into any such theological folly. Obviously, this would also include following him into apostasy or apathy. You do not have the excuse that you stopped going to church because your husband did. Neither of you may forsake the gathering of the saints, but if a husband does, a godly wife carries on attending in obedience to Christ. That is what a godly wife's *submission* looks like in those difficult circumstances. This is because a Christian woman knows that she was created for infinite glory. She knows what she is becoming, and so she is practicing for that glory now.

QUESTIONS FOR DISCUSSION

1. *What does submission "in the Lord" mean for any authority or inferior?*

2. *What does "delegated" or "derivative" authority mean?*

3. *What are the two categories where a woman may gladly submit to her husband in the Lord?*

4. *In what area does Christian submission require a woman not to obey her husband? What are some of the common areas where this can creep in?*

5. *What should a Christian wife or any Christian under authority do when the authority is requiring disobedience to God's law?*

CHAPTER 6

DON'T SHIPWRECK
THE HEADSHIP

"For the husband is the head of the wife, even as Christ is the head of the church: and he is the saviour of the body" (Eph. 5:23).

We have covered a good bit of what it means for a wife to submit to her own husband in the Lord. But what does it mean that a husband is the "head" of his wife? What should a man be aiming at? And what should a wife be praying for? You should think of at least three words when you think of "head" or "headship": representative, responsibility, and leader.

First, Paul is clearly using an anatomical analogy, and this relates to the idea of *representation*. When you talk to someone, you generally talk to their face, to their head. Their hands and knees are just as much part of them as their head and face, but the face represents them to the world. It would be very strange to talk to someone's elbow when carrying on a conversation. This is clearly designed by God in the natural sensory features located on the face: eyes, ears, mouth, and nose. Even though God is infinite and does not have a body like men, friendship with God is described as "face to face" (Exod. 33:11). Love, to know and be known fully, is a "face to face" reality (1 Cor. 13:12). And every Christian's greatest hope and longing is to see Christ as He is, and when we see Him, we will be like Him (1 Jn. 3:2). But there is much more going on than a mere anatomical analogy. This is covenantal language. How is a husband to think of himself as being the head of his wife? Paul tells us: "as Christ is the head of the church, the saviour of the body."

This is not just a passing metaphor. This is a repeated theme: Jesus is called the "head of the body, the church" in Colossians (Col. 1:18). Jesus is also called the "head" of the Church earlier in the book of Ephesians: "And hath put all things under his feet, and gave him to be the head over all things to the church, which is his body, the fulness of him that filleth all in all" (Eph. 1:22–23). Here we see that Christ's covenantal headship means that Christ rules all things for the blessing of the Church, which is his body, and the Church in turn is the fullness of Christ. There is a sense in which the Church represents Christ and proclaims Christ to the world, but there is actually a far more important sense in which Christ represents us. He is our image, the immortal image we are growing up into. Again in Ephesians, "But speaking the truth in love, [we] may grow up into him in all things, which is the head, even Christ: from whom the whole body fitly joined together and compacted by that which every joint supplieth, according to the effectual working in the measure of every part, maketh increase of the body unto the edifying of itself in love" (Eph. 4:15–16). Here Paul says that the body—the Church—is growing up into Christ our head, and we do that by receiving our gifting and assignments from our head.

A husband is called to imitate this headship for his wife, and while there is certainly a mutual encouragement between the spouses toward growth in holiness, the husband is called to imitate the example of Christ in particular, as the head of his wife. Incidentally, this means that he is to set the example of speaking truth in love, growing in holiness, so that his wife is being edified in love and being supplied with the encouragement and resources to grow up into Christ. If a man notices something lacking in his wife, the first place he should check is himself. What example is he setting? What kind of image is he presenting for her to follow, for her to imitate? A selfish husband will tend to cultivate (surprise!) a selfish wife. Being the head of his wife means that he has been tasked with being one of the great sources of strength and power to grow in love. Paul says that the body is growing up into its head, from which the body is being "fitly joined together." So being the head and representative of your wife in part means that you are called to image what she is supposed to grow up into in Christ. And, men, that should terrify you (in a good way). And the only hope either of you have for this to go well is if Christ is your head.

So Jesus is our head and representative. His great act of representation was on the cross when He stood in our place, the righteous for the unrighteous (1 Pet. 3:18). He does this now in Heaven with the Father. He intercedes for us as our High Priest (Heb. 2:17, 7:25). Likewise, He represents the Father to us. If you have seen Jesus, you have seen the Father (Jn. 14:9). This whole concept of representation is actually directly connected to the biblical concept of *covenant*, and covenant is at the center of the Christian gospel. One of the easiest ways to get to the heart of this concept is by asking how Adam's sin has affected the human race. How was it that by one man, six thousand years ago, sin came upon all men, as Paul says in Romans 5:18? Does that seem fair or just? The only way this would be fair is if Adam was our "head," our *covenantal* head. It would only make sense if Adam *represented* all of us. And so he did represent us, such that his personal sin was also a public sin that entailed all of his descendants. This is what theologians call "original sin."

But the glory of the gospel is that Jesus is our new Adam. His personal obedience was also a public, covenantal obedience for all those who put their trust in Him: "For if by one man's offence death reigned by one; much more they which receive abundance of grace and of the gift of righteousness shall reign in life by one, Jesus Christ. Therefore as by the offence of one judgment came upon all men to condemnation; even so by the righteousness of one the free gift came upon all men unto justification of life" (Rom. 5:17–18).

So a man is called to imitate *that* kind of covenantal love with his wife and children (or is preparing to). "Husbands, love your wives, even as Christ also loved the church, and gave himself for it" (Eph. 5:25). How are husbands to love their wives? *Covenantally*, like Jesus did. We may as well add here that the Bible explicitly says that marriage is a covenant relationship. This is implied in Proverbs: "To deliver thee from the strange woman, even from the stranger which flattereth with her words; which forsaketh the guide of her youth, and forgetteth the *covenant* of her God" (Prov. 2:16–17, emphasis mine). What is the adulterous woman forgetting? She is forgetting the *covenant* she made before God with her husband. We see the same thing even more explicitly in Malachi:

> Yet ye say, Wherefore? Because the LORD hath been witness between thee and the wife of thy youth, against whom thou hast dealt treacherously: yet is she thy companion, and the wife of thy *covenant*. And did not he make one? Yet had he the residue of the spirit. And wherefore one? That he might seek a godly seed. Therefore, take heed to your spirit, and let none deal treacherously against the wife of his youth. For the LORD, the God of Israel, saith that he hateth putting away: for one covereth violence with his garment, saith the LORD of hosts: therefore take heed to your spirit, that ye deal not treacherously. (Mal. 2:14–16, emphasis mine)

Here Malachi explains God's displeasure with the Jews specifically for how they have been treacherous to their marriage vows, for breaking the marriage covenant through divorce and covering themselves with violence. And the violence comes from separating what God has made into one. In the beginning, God made the man that he might leave his father and mother and be united to his wife such that the two might become one flesh. That one flesh union is what we call a covenantal union. A man can represent his wife because he is united to her in the covenant of marriage. His love can be Christ-like and efficacious in drawing his wife closer to Christ and Christ-likeness and can truly minister to his wife's needs because they are covenantally united.

But all of this underlines the disastrous effects of breaking the marriage covenant. The Bible does acknowledge the sad necessity and lawfulness of divorce in some instances, but God hates divorce, and many people can testify to the harsh and bitter consequences of many divorces that initially promised peace and comfort. Countless millions of children have borne the violence of these rifts, growing up in single-parent—often single-mother—families, actually or functionally fatherless. Rising rates of violence and drug use and suicide are not unrelated to the breakdown of the family. All statistics consistently demonstrate stability, joy, and peace in children from intact marriages. But the violence goes much further. In a culture of mass divorce, is it really any surprise that we have simultaneously murdered millions by abortion? Sometimes abortion has been the direct result of sexual infidelity and adultery, attempts at covering sin at the expense of innocent little ones, but the point is not merely a directly causative one. The point is also related to cultural momentum and secondary consequences: mass divorce is an attack on marriage as an institution. It renders marriage insecure and unsafe, and, therefore the one place where new immortal people are meant by God to be welcomed and protected no longer exists. You cannot break covenant vows easily and expect there to be no consequences. This is because the marriage covenant is a picture of God's love for His people, a sign of the New Covenant and Christ's efficacious and permanent love for His bride, the Church. Every husband represents Christ in this way as the covenant head of his wife. You cannot tear a husband and wife apart without extreme consequences.

The covenantal nature of marriage is why ordinarily the husband is the spokesperson for the family. He should learn to use the first person plural: *we*. We think, we believe, we love, we hate. He speaks before the world on behalf of his family, and he speaks to God on behalf of his family. This doesn't mean that a Christian wife hides in the shadows or that she may never speak in public. It just means that, ordinarily, he's the spokesperson. He is the head; he is the designated representative. And it should be a normal, glorious thing for a wife to say, "My husband says ..."

This is not at all related to natural speaking abilities. God did not make men the head of the marriage covenant and the spokesmen for their households because they are better public speakers. Many men are not as quick with words or as articulate as their wives, and yet they are still assigned the task of representing their household. And this duty really isn't interchangeable based on gifts, interests, or abilities. This task of representing a wife and family to God and the world is given to the man because it is part of protecting his wife and family and taking responsibility for them. If you have a very low view of what the family is for, this may seem rather random and capricious. *Hey, how come he gets to speak for us?* But if you understand that God is doing something significant with the family, that the stakes are really high—we are making immortals—suddenly, we may be more comfortable with God assigning the man to be the spokesman.

This task of being spokesman is not something a man can just wing. In that great Christian calendar verse, Joshua famously said, "Choose you this day whom ye will serve ... as for me and my house, we will serve the LORD" (Josh. 24:15). Now that sounds all pious and brave (and it really was), but I don't think many Christians, particularly Christian men, spend enough time contemplating what this statement means.

As this is the end of Joshua's life (he died at 110 years old), there were no doubt at least four, maybe five generations below him as he spoke to the heads of Israel. If Joshua and his children were all monogamous, each marriage had only five kids per marriage, and each generation was divided by about eighteen years (all very conservative estimates, it seems to me), Joshua could have been speaking on behalf of over three thousand grandchildren. And if ancient mortality rates would seem to make that number too high, let's cut it down to just one thousand descendants alive while Joshua is speaking. That's still a very large household that Joshua is *representing*.

The question for our purposes is: Is Joshua representing his household *well*? Is he speaking on behalf of his family accurately? The question is not whether Joshua *means* well. The question is whether Joshua actually *knows* what he's talking about. Will his household *actually* serve the Lord? A good representative *represents* and speaks for his people well because he *knows* his people well and has led his people well. The task of spokesman and representative is an assignment to study and teach.

In other words, Joshua is either an egregious example of male hubris and presumption, e.g., "I'm the boss and I can I talk this way because my family orbits around my ego." Or else this is an example of deep humility and courage. Either Joshua was an incredibly arrogant man caught up in the hyper-patriarchal spirit of the age, or else Joshua was being a faithful and godly *man*. Since we have every reason to believe that this was Joshua finishing his ministry strong, Joshua must have been speaking accurately about his household. Joshua was able to make this faithful and courageous stand before the elders of Israel because he had been a faithful head of his household, diligently speaking to them, teaching them, and leading them to serve the Lord. Joshua could speak this way because he had lived this way. He knew what he was talking about. Every man who says "I do" is promising to think and speak and live this way, beginning with his wife.

This notion of covenant *representation* leads directly to the second word we mentioned at the beginning of this chapter: *responsibility*. Responsibility is something that God assigns, which is to say that it is the flip side of the coin of authority. You cannot have authority without responsibility. If God assigns responsibility, then He is also bestowing authority. But since our first father's sin, men have been responsibility evaders. Adam blamed Eve (and implicitly God) for his sin: "the woman you gave me ..." Then Cain did the same when God confronted him about Abel's death: "Am I my brother's keeper?" And so on, down through male history. We want the authority without the responsibility. We want the right to command without the liability of any consequences. But this is necessarily to shipwreck the headship. The right to command includes with it the liability for disaster. If you order the ship towards an island and tear open the hull on a hidden reef, that is your fault, O Captain. You are responsible.

This is part of what Paul means when he says that husbands are to love their wives "even as Christ loved the church and gave himself for it; that he might sanctify and cleanse it with the washing of water by the word, that he might present it to himself a glorious church, not having spot, or wrinkle, or any such thing; but that it should be holy and without blemish. So ought men to love their wives as their own bodies" (Eph. 5:25–28). Jesus took responsibility for His bride the Church and died *for* her sins. He *represented* us in His death, and He did so well by taking *responsibility* for us and our sins. A Christian husband does not lay his life down for his wife in the exact same way—a fallen man, no matter how good his intentions, cannot *pay* for the sins of his wife. Only a perfect sacrifice can atone for our sins. But nevertheless, the Bible clearly commands husbands to *imitate* this kind of love. A Christian husband cannot save his wife from her sins, but a Christian husband is to labor to sacrificially love and lead his wife with the goal of sanctification and purity. This command implies that real results are possible. The command clearly implies that it is entirely possible for a fallen man, by the grace of God, to love his wife in a way that makes her more holy and more lovely. This is what we mean by *efficacious* love—a love that effects real holiness and beauty—a holiness and beauty that will be raised from the dead and live forever. This means that a Christian husband must view any weaknesses, spots, or wrinkles as *his* problem. This is what it means to be the "head" of his wife and to take responsibility for her. This does not eradicate a woman's personal responsibility before God, her personal agency for her choices, and her personal guilt for her own sins, but marriage is a real covenant with a head who is responsible for his wife just like he is responsible for the rest of his body.

Jesus was the only perfect man in the history of the world, and He who knew no sin became sin for us (covenantally), so that we might become the righteousness of God in Him (2 Cor. 5:21). If any man had the right to blame someone else, it was Christ, but instead of pointing fingers, He took responsibility. He took the burden that we created, but He took our burden in an efficacious way, in a truly effective way, in a way that took away our sin and delivered us from the power of evil. This is the kind of love husbands are commanded to imitate. This is not a vacuous, mindless, lay-down-and-take-it "love." This is not sentimental, do-whatever-she-says "love." A husband is not commanded to submit to his wife. Rather, he is commanded to love her like Christ loved us. She is an immortal soul, a woman made in the image of the Living God destined for immortality, and you are called to love her toward the glory of holiness. That doesn't mean doing whatever she wants. It means doing whatever God says she needs.

Job is one of the great examples of taking familial responsibility in Scripture. "And it was so, when the days of [his sons'] feasting were gone about, that Job sent and sanctified them, and rose up early in the morning, and offered burnt offerings according to the number of them all: for Job said, it may be that my sons have sinned, and cursed God in their hearts. Thus did Job continually" (Job 1:5). Here, Job offered sacrifices to God on behalf of his sons who *might* have sinned in their hearts.

This is what responsibility does. It owns God's design of influence. By God's design, influence can and does flow in many different directions: a Christian woman can have a sanctifying influence on her unbelieving husband (cf. 1 Cor. 7:14). But the natural gravity of the world includes the influence of authority and hierarchy, and with authority comes responsibility. A husband has a God-assigned influence on his wife. This means that when a man sees a weakness or sin in his wife, he should begin by looking at himself *first*. Are there ways that you are sinning? Are you being lazy or indifferent or cowardly in your work, in your walk with the Lord, or in your leadership of your wife? This is partially an application of the Lord's instruction to remove the log from your own eye first (Matt. 7:3–5), but this is also a straightforward application of the covenantal head-body theology. A man's disobedience has a disproportionate negative effect on his wife and family, but by the same token a man's humble obedience has a disproportionate positive effect on his wife and family. This really is a point of encouragement. Men can do great damage by their sin and negligence, but by the grace of God, when a man repents all the way down to the ground and truly humbles himself before God, the whole family can feel that and sense that something really is different. If you have not been faithful at your post, confess your sin to God, to your wife, and your children, and get back to work. You are the head of your wife, the head of your household, and God has designed His grace to flow from you to your whole family.

Are you seeking the Lord for your wife or wife-to-be? Are you confessing your own sins regularly? Are you confessing the sins of your household, or preparing to? Are you confessing in the first person plural, "Father, we have sinned ..."? And if you are still preparing to do that, are you taking responsibility now at work, at church, in your neighborhood—seeing needs and problems and running toward them with solutions? Or do you say, *That's not my problem. Am I my brother's keeper? Not my circus, not my monkeys.* There is a sort of meddling that really is grabbing a stray dog by the ears, which must be avoided, but most men struggle far more with actually taking responsibility than they do with meddling. And when men are meddling, they are frequently doing so as a distraction tactic from their own responsibilities. But you are standing on the brink of eternity. This life will be like a brief shadow compared to the glory of the resurrection. What are you building? What are you becoming? Where are you taking your people?

QUESTIONS FOR DISCUSSION

1. *What is the image that Paul uses to describe the role of the husband? And what are some of the things this implies?*

2. *How does a man represent his wife/family well? How would a man represent his wife/family poorly?*

3. *What does it mean for a man to take responsibility for his wife? What are men tempted to do with their wives' weaknesses or sins?*

4. *How is a Christian man commanded to love his wife? What is the standard for evaluating how a man is doing?*

5. *How does a Christian man pray before God for his wife/family?*

CHAPTER 7

GOING INTO THE FIRE FIRST

"For the husband is the head of the wife, even as Christ is the head of the church: and he is saviour of the body ... Husbands, love your wives, even as Christ loved the church, and gave himself for it" (Eph. 5:23, 25).

Another picture the Bible gives us of what it means for a man to be the "head" of his wife is found in the sacrificial system. And this is where we begin pressing into that third word (mentioned at the beginning of the last chapter) that you need to think of when you consider what it means to be the head, and that's the word "leader." When an animal was brought to the tabernacle or temple to be offered, the worshiper laid his hands on the *head* of the animal, designating the animal as his representative, likely confessing his sins as he did so (Lev.

1:4, cf. Lev. 16:21–22). Then, in the case of the ascension offering (sometimes translated "whole burnt offering") the animal was butchered, and the head and entrails were immediately put on the altar in the fire to ascend to God in smoke (Lev. 1:8, 12, cf. Exod. 29:15–18).

This is one of the images a husband ought to have *in* his head when thinking about what it means to *be* the head of his wife. This sacrificial image is ultimately pointing to Jesus who became our sin offering, our sacrifice for sin. He took our place and went into the fire of God's judgment for sin instead of us. But there is another sense in which everyone will go into God's fire—because our God *is* a consuming fire. The question is not whether we will pass through the fire of God's presence, the question is whether we will survive the experience. Christ took the hellfire of God's judgment for us, His people, so that we might pass through God's holiness-fire and survive. Christ had to go into the fire first; otherwise, we'd have all been burnt to a crisp. Paul says that husbands are to love their wives like this. Husbands do this by taking responsibility for their wives, considering the challenges, weaknesses, and sins of their wives as their responsibility, their problem to solve, their assignment from God. This is lived out by standing between your wife and the various social, spiritual, medical, vocational, emotional, philosophical, cultural, and moral "fires" that threaten her. A Christian man seeks to go into the fire first, making a path for his wife to follow.

Most men have a deep protective instinct that makes them ready and eager to defend their wife from immediate physical danger. If someone breaks into their home in the middle of the night, most men have a knee-jerk *over-my-dead-body* reaction. It is the glory and honor of men to stand between their women and danger. But many men who would otherwise make excellent heroes in a shootout are oblivious to the many other kinds of bullets flying at their woman. These may come in the form of toxic friend-ships, difficulties with the kids, bad attitudes, the dishes, poor entertainment choices, financial stress, cultural lies, vocational burdens, spiritual immaturity, or health prob-lems—and frequently combinations of all of the above. These bullets are just as nasty and threatening, but they are harder to spot and harder still to take. The point is not that everything a woman may *think* is a threat to her sanity and spiritual well-being actually is a threat, but that you are responsible for her well-being and safety. Sometimes you will need to step in and assist or intervene if there's a diffi-cult interpersonal situation. But a wise man wants to actu-ally protect his wife and not shelter her or belittle her. This means that he must *love* her. He must love her as his own body. He must know her frame, understand her concerns, and carefully lead her to be more and more faithful, more and more like Christ, and he must do so with *diligence*.

I remember learning this principle—somewhat acciden-tally (by the grace of God)—in the early years of our mar-riage when we had a medical situation where bills began arriving in the tens and hundreds of thousands of dollars. Thankfully we had decent health insurance, but thus began a part-time job of making phone calls with hospitals, doc-tors' offices, and health insurance companies, making sure that bills were correct, insurance claims had been coded correctly, and payments had actually been recorded. While my wife had been our family bookkeeper for years, and she dutifully began the work of making the phone calls and tracking all the numbers, I asked her one day if she'd like me to do it for her, and she immediately and enthusiastically welcomed the suggestion. In fact, her enthusiasm was a little convicting. She likely could have done the work, but it really was sort of stressful and tedious and would have been the sort of thing that would have hung on her a lot more heavily and might have kept her up at night. That's just one low-level example of standing between a wife and a potential danger (administrative stress, financial stress), but hopefully it gives you something to talk about with your wife or fiancée. What sorts of things stress your woman out or tempt her that way? Maybe loving leadership will mean that over time some of those stresses need to be faced and simply conquered. My point isn't that a good husband takes over anything that is hard for his wife to do. Love is committed to seeing the object of your love grow in godliness and holiness and maturity. But the point is that a man who wants to love a woman well needs to know where all the fires are in her life, where the threats are, and he must take responsibility for her and go into the fire for her. Sometimes you will need to pull her out of the fire, and sometimes you will need to stand there with her and teach her how to fight the fire faithfully. But playing the man means that you are promising to go into the fire *first*.

Paul underlines the fact that Adam was created first as a good reason to prohibit women from teaching men in the Church or having authority over men (1 Tim.

2:12–13). Those who want to argue that Paul is address-ing a specific cultural moment in Ephesus really have a problem, given that Paul grounds his reason in creation itself—this is how God made the world. Paul underlines the same point elsewhere: "For the man is not of the woman; but the woman of the man. Neither was the man created for the woman; but the woman for the man" (1 Cor. 11:8–9). But while the feminists and egalitarians hy-perventilate into bags, we can draw some very profitable truth from this glorious reality, the central thing being the *process* by which God created the woman. "And the Lord God caused a deep sleep to fall upon Adam, and he slept: and he took one of his ribs, and closed up the flesh instead thereof; and the rib, which the Lord God had taken from man, made he a woman, and brought her unto the man" (Gen. 2:21–22).

While the Lord was kind enough to provide anesthe-sia for this operation, it is worth noting that this was the first major surgery in the history of the world. This sur-gery included breaking one of Adam's rib bones off of his rib cage and sewing his chest cavity back up. We can rest assured that this surgery was a complete success, but we really shouldn't skate over these details. Adam was created first, and this was so that he could be cut open first. Adam had to be cut open first before the woman could be created. We can actually see this same pattern in the entire creation week: God creates something and then breaks it in half or divides it in some fashion in order to make something new. He divided the light from the darkness to create day and night (Gen. 1:4–5). He divided the waters above from the waters below to create the firmament (Gen. 1:6–7). He gathered all the waters under Heaven together, dividing them from the dry ground, creating the earth and the seas (Gen. 1:9–10). And now here, God breaks Adam open and divides a rib from his body in order to create the woman.

This is also what it means to be the "head" of your wife, what it means to be the leader. To be the head, to be first, is to be broken open first, to be cut first, for the good of your bride, for the sake of your bride. "And Adam said, this is now bone of my bones, and flesh of my flesh: she shall be called Woman, because she was taken out of Man. Therefore shall a man leave his father and his mother, and shall cleave unto his wife: and they shall be one flesh" (Gen. 2:23–24). Why do people get married? They get married because woman was taken out of man, because the first man was put into a deep sleep and God fashioned the woman from his rib. In Ephesians 5, Paul says that this is talking about Christ and the Church and it is a great mystery, but given the clear pattern of Adam and Eve and Christ and the Church, we may safely say that to become a husband is to promise to die for your bride, to promise to be cut open for her, to suffer for her, to take great pain gladly so that she will be all lovely, all glorious, without spot or wrinkle or any blemish.

The image of head and body is also helpful in thinking about what leadership looks like. Most people have experienced something of what this is like in athletics. Begin with the best coaches. Coaches push you beyond what you think you are capable of because they have a goal in mind that you cannot imagine. The best coaches make you hurt, but they make you hurt with understanding. They know what your body can take, and you are so grateful after the fact. You would never push yourself so hard on your own, but it is a great gift to be pushed beyond what you think you can handle by someone who is committed to making you better. No discipline is pleasant for the moment, but the fruit of discipline is glorious. When you're winning that gold medal, that championship, you are so grateful for that coach. This is what a faithful husband does as the head of his wife—but this means, to preview another text we will get to shortly, husbands must "dwell with them according to knowledge" (1 Pet. 3:7). Just as a good coach must remember the frame of their athlete, so too a wise husband must know what his wife can handle. It is not enough to assert that he is the leader or that it is for her good. He must actually see her flourishing under his leadership. He is called by God to lead his wife to become more godly, more holy, more pure, more industrious, through his cheering, leading, and loving.

Extend the analogy in a different direction, still having to do with athletics. Most athletics requires a "head game" or "mental game," where an athlete has to have a sturdy and clear-thinking mind to govern all of his or her strategy, feelings, aches, pains, etc. That clear mind must also be truly sensible and knowledgeable of the body. Paul says that a man should think of his care for his wife just as he thinks of his care for his own body. "For no man ever yet hated his own flesh; but nourisheth and cherisheth it, even as the Lord the church" (Eph. 5:29).

I remember in high school going out for varsity soccer my sophomore year. The late August Maryland heat and humidity were intense, even with practices in the mornings. When I was cut from the team after a month or so of practices, my buddy talked me into running cross-country, since I was "already in shape." Ha. Turns out running cross-country was a little different than running suicides for soccer. At my first practice, the coach announced we were doing something like a ten-mile run. I think I made it to mile four or so before I nearly collapsed, sure I was dying (okay, maybe I am being a little dramatic). Thus began the challenge of not only getting my body and lungs into better shape, but also getting my mind into shape.

As you work at any sort of endurance sport, your mind (and body) will tell you truths, partial truths, half lies, and outright lies. Your lungs say they are about to collapse; your side aches and screams and says you're going to die. Your legs and feet also send up their objections. You begin to wonder if this is really all that necessary. Do you really believe in this? Couldn't you sleep in today? Couldn't you call it quits at half the workout and try again tomorrow? You didn't get great sleep last night after all ... and the excuses creep in and multiply (if you let them). Your mind, your *head*, has to sort through it all. A great deal of what you have to tell your body and those doubts and excuses is that everything is going to be okay. Keep going; don't give up. On the other hand, a certain kind of sharp pain shooting from your Achilles really must be addressed, sometimes your lungs are telling the truth; sometimes you really are coming down with the flu. But what is love in this situation? Love is listening to your body, telling your body the truth (in love), cheering your body on, while pushing it to its maximum potential. Love doesn't mean doing whatever your body says. If that were love, there would be no athletes and certainly no long-distance runners.

"Know ye not that they which run in a race run all, but one receiveth the prize? So run, that ye may obtain. And every man that striveth for the mastery is temperate in all things. Now they do it to obtain a corruptible crown; but we an incorruptible. I therefore so run, not as uncertainly; so fight I, not as one that beateth the air: But I keep under my body, and bring it into subjection: lest that by any means, when I have preached to others, I myself should be a castaway" (1 Cor. 9:24–27). If Paul says that a man ought to love his wife as his own body, then this passage applies to how a husband thinks about *how* he is to love his wife. He is to love her with the same holy ambition and determination he is to have for himself: temperance in all things, aiming for an incorruptible crown, preaching the gospel everywhere and in everything. This also means that this is hard work and something that takes constant maintenance, endurance, and joy, with eyes fixed on the prize. A husband is not an ordained pastor, but he certainly has pastoral duties toward his wife. He is called to lead her to Christ, to coach her towards holiness and wisdom, to disciple her into the glorious image of Jesus, all situated in and through her duties as a wife, a mother, and a home manager, and in every area of life: Bible study, prayer, friendship, entertainment, and so on.

I remember toward the end of that cross-country season coming home one Saturday after a race—3.1 miles (5K). I wasn't a particularly fast runner, probably a little farther back than the middle of the pack, but I remember the feeling of coming home, feeling great, feeling energized, and suddenly the most absurd thought occurred to me: *I could do that again.* I'm pretty sure that was the high-water mark of my physical fitness for my whole life. And thus ended my illustrious career in cross-country. But the point is that people can and do get into shape with lots of joyful, thoughtful discipline and practice.

This principle applies to spiritual self-discipline (1 Cor. 9:27), but the principle also applies to marriage. The husband is required by God to love his wife as Christ loves the Church, laying his life down for her, washing her with the water of the Word, with the goal of her *complete* sanctification. And a man is required by God to consider this a form of godly self-love and self-discipline (Eph. 5:26–28). If a man would push himself to lift weights, run long distances, read fat books, fix his car, build a house, run a business, he ought to have at the top of his list (right below his own pursuit of Christ) loving his wife into a perfect and glorious image of Christ. But if the pattern is the self-sacrifice of Christ on the cross, and nature itself teaches us that self-discipline is difficult but very rewarding, this task of loving one woman with dedication, with this purpose is a task of no small magnitude, but the returns are magnificent. A husband must diligently know the state of his wife and with biblical kindness and courage lead her daily into greater and greater faithfulness in every area of life. Coasting is not an option.

"Therefore as the church is subject unto Christ, so let the wives be to their own husbands in every thing" (Eph. 5:24). While a wise man will not micromanage his wife and will gladly delegate many responsibilities to his wife, Paul here clearly says "in every thing," which is to say that he is responsible for all of it and may not shirk his responsibility by saying he didn't know or that's *her* business. No, you will answer to God for all of it. Obviously, if you are preparing to be married, your fiancée has not yet entrusted everything to you, and so you are not yet authorized to inquire into everything. But you are practicing for that day, and you should know what it is that you are practicing for. If you're already married, you have no excuses, man.

Lastly, a *living* head must have a *living* body. Not to put too fine a point on it, a head without a body is, well, *dead*. What I mean is that men ought to think of their task as the head of their wife as being something like leading a safari through a rainforest jungle. Because, I mean, what man doesn't secretly wish he were going on a safari through a rainforest jungle most days? Well, actually, if you're thinking accurately and soberly about the threat of sin, your mission as a husband, and the work before you, it's not really that different. On the one hand, you really do need to go first into the jungle of life, and you need to go first because you're the man and your job is to die first, to lay your life down first, to get cut first. You go first so that you will fall into the quicksand instead of her, so that you will lose your footing instead of her, so that you will encounter the poisonous snake instead of her.

However, this task of going first, of leading, means that it is not enough for you to merely go first and shout out warnings behind you carelessly. Your job is to go first and then to make sure that she is following well. A man cannot march off into the jungles barking commands and then look behind him three hours later and wonder why she isn't there. That man is no leader, whatever he calls himself. A leader *leads*, and a leader keeps track of those he is leading. He announces the low hanging branch— "watch your head here!" and holds it up, looking back to make sure she managed it well. If your wife needs to go slower in order to make it alive, then you must go slower. If your wife needs more help, then you must give it. "Leave no man behind" has been an unofficial rallying cry of valor for various military units and soldiers. Too many Christian men have not had that same code of honor with their own wives (or children). A godly head stays in tune with his body. A godly head spends time and energy faithfully, prayerfully, and carefully leading his family to follow his convictions, and in so doing, he is shaping immortal souls and building a legacy that will last forever.

QUESTIONS FOR DISCUSSION

1. What does the sacrificial system teach us about what it means to be the "head" in marriage?

2. Why was Adam created first? What practical implications flow from that fact?

3. How is headship like good coaching?

4. How does the "mental game" involved in athletics help inform what a godly husband, as the head, must do to love his wife?

5. The Bible teaches that a wife must submit to her husband "in every thing"—what does that indicate about a husband's duty toward his wife?

CHAPTER 8

THE WATER OF THE WORD

B IBLICAL headship is also closely related to "the washing of water by the word" (Eph. 5:26). How does
Jesus sanctify and cleanse His bride? *By His Word.* His
Word washes His bride clean. And this is the example
for Christian husbands to follow. Obviously this means
being men of the Word. Read the Bible. Study the Bible.
Memorize the Bible. Sing the Bible. Talk about the Bible. Much of the most important washing by the Word
in a family doesn't occur at planned or set times, so you
need to be prepared. You can't wash with the Word if you
aren't dripping with Bible.

It is good to have rhythms of personal devotions and
family worship, and times to read the Bible and pray as
a couple, but you also want to be marinating in the Bible

throughout the day and throughout the week. When you're helping with the dishes and you're talking about what so-and-so said on Facebook, you really want to be able to "wash" that moment and situation with the Word of God. What does God say about that comment she made about her husband? What does the Bible say about our financial situation? What does the *Word* say about our plans? When one of the kids do something troubling, you want to be able to encourage your wife and apply the water of the Word to that situation. Washing with the Word should be thorough and regular. Think of it like marinating meat. You want to be soaking in the Word of God constantly. Share what you've read, ask questions that you're pondering, sing the Psalms together, stop and pray in the middle of things, acknowledging that you need the Lord's guidance and care in everything, all the time. Because you do.

A man also needs to recognize that his authority is grounded in the Word of God. Therefore, a great deal of a man's leadership in his home should begin with the words, "The Bible says ..." In doing this a man is reinforcing the fact that his authority is *derived* from the Lord. A man receives his authority from God, and therefore, he should be regularly referring to *his* head, *his* boss. Of course, a man can say these words in a condescending or crushing way, but when he does it in the right spirit, it is entirely comforting and reassuring to his wife and family. A man who never refers to his head is teaching his family that he got his authority out of thin air all by himself. This is not only a great way to make everyone feel insecure; it's also a great way to teach everyone that it's perfectly fine to conjure up authority out of thin air, including right now when I don't feel like obeying you.

One of the most important ways a man takes responsibility for the spiritual growth and nurture of his wife is by committing to membership in a local church. While private and family Bible reading and worship are important, the worship of the Church on the Lord's Day is central. Jesus did not give the keys of the Kingdom, the duty to proclaim the gospel and baptize the nations, to husbands or fathers. Jesus gave the keys of the Kingdom to the Church, to elders and pastors who stand on the shoulders of the apostles and prophets (Matt. 16:18–19, 18:15–20; Eph. 4:11–13). This ministry of the local church does not replace the true ministry of a husband and father in his home, but rather it is an essential part of that true ministry. A man who does not prioritize weekly gathered worship with the body of Christ is an arrogant man, pretending that he knows better than Jesus. Furthermore, a man who refuses to submit himself to a local session of elders is often not to be a trusted leader himself. All biblical authority is delegated and derived authority. There is no authority except from God (Rom. 13:1). Godly authorities demonstrate that they understand this by submitting to other lawful, God-ordained authorities in those areas where God has granted them jurisdiction. The man who will not submit to biblical Church authority or lawful civil authority should not be trusted with familial authority. This is also why it is always good to see a man with his parents before promising to marry him. A man who has a solid, respectful relationship with his parents demonstrates that he understands authority biblically. But if a man is headstrong and constantly bucking biblical authority, no Christian woman should go near him.

Since we live in the Wild West days of Church membership, and many churches no longer even practice such a thing, and therefore many true hearted Christians don't even know what "membership" in a local church means, let me just sketch it for you briefly. The basic case for membership in a local church (and not just general membership in the universal body of Christ) is found in Hebrews 13. Here the apostle says that Christians must remember the elders that "rule over you, who have spoken the word of God: whose faith follow, considering the end of their conversation" (Heb. 13:7). This clearly means that Christians must know particular men who preach to them and teach them the Word. Christians should know them well enough to watch their "conversation," which is Old King James for knowing what flavor of ice cream they prefer. If you're not close enough to your elders to watch the outcome of their lives, to see how they interact with their wives and children, you aren't doing it right.

A little further down, it says, "Obey them that have the rule over you, and submit yourselves: for they watch for your souls, as they that must give an account, that they may do it with joy, and not with grief: for that is unprofitable for you" (Heb. 13:17). Christians must not only remember and know their elders, but they must submit to them and obey them. This may seem as patriarchal and medieval as a wife submitting to her own husband and taking a vow of obedience to him, and it is—positively

medieval, gloriously medieval. But even more importantly, it is glorious and wholesome and pleasing to the Lord.
Furthermore, we are told that elders are those who must
give an account for particular people. So the bottom line
is that Church membership is simply the practice of being in submission to particular elders who teach you the
Word and obeying them, and particular elders knowing
which Christians they are responsible for and ministering in such a way as to be prepared to give a faithful
account for them to the Lord. There is no one particular
way to carry this out, but generally, you will need to have
two lists of names somewhere: a list of elders and a list
of members. Finally, this rule in the Church includes the
duty of Church discipline, of adjudicating matters of sin
and disputes, making rulings, and, where there is refusal
to repent of sin, excommunication—putting people outside the church (Matt. 18:15–20, 1 Cor. 5:1–13).

I fully realize that it is not always possible to be part
of a faithful church that recognizes or performs all of
these duties. But biblical wisdom prioritizes the ministry of the local church and seeks out the best Christian
fellowship that can be found, a fellowship committed to
the preaching and teaching the Word of God. On the one
hand, don't despise a good option simply because you
can't find the best option, the most ideal. In other words,
don't be a perfectionist. On the other hand, if a suitable
fellowship cannot be found locally, a godly man really
must take responsibility for this major problem and likely
make some drastic decisions about his work and living
situation. Hopefully, as you have talked about preparing

for marriage, where you will worship has been just as central to all the rest of your plans about where you will live and work, etc. If this has not been central to your conversations, you should start making it central. You would never take a job across the country and get in a moving van and say that you'll figure out where you'll live when you get there. If you wouldn't do that with living arrangements, why would you do that with worship and Church membership? This is a central duty of Christians, and it is a central duty of a married man to provide for his wife so that she is being washed in the water by the Word.

We have already touched on Paul's instruction that a husband must "nourish and cherish" his wife just as Christ does the Church. But one more thing really must be stated explicitly. The words "nourish and cherish" literally mean "feed and keep warm." We noted earlier that Paul is likely echoing the words of Exodus 21:10 that establish the bare minimum a woman can justly require of her husband. Likewise, Paul tells Timothy, "But if any provide not for his own, and specially for those of his own house, he hath denied the faith, and is worse than an infidel" (1 Tim. 5:8). Putting these texts together, it really must be insisted that a man must be the breadwinner of his family, the one who provides and protects his family and failure to do so is tantamount to apostasy. In other words, a "stay-at-home dad" is a shameful abomination. Given the world we live in, for some, this statement may seem painfully obvious and for others I may have just poked you bluntly in the eye, but I want to explain this carefully and clearly because you are preparing for marriage in a world that has gone mad on these matters, and so this really does need to be understood biblically.

While the Bible certainly does not prohibit a woman from making money or having a job—the Proverbs 31 wife is a prolifically industrious and successful business-woman—the Bible is clear that a woman's greatest glory is making a home. A godly woman's industry and creativity and vocational pursuits should be oriented to her central vocation of being a homemaker and, as God blesses, a wife and a mother. Her industry and business endeavors should be directed to the blessing of her husband and children: "The heart of her husband doth safely trust in her ... she will do him good and not evil all the days of her life ... she looketh well to the ways of her household ... Her children arise up, and call her blessed; her husband also, and he praiseth her" (Prov. 31:11–12, 27–28). Likewise, Paul instructs Titus that older women are to teach younger women to "be sober, to love their husbands, to love their children, to be discreet, chaste, keepers at home, good, obedient to their own husbands, that the word of God be not blasphemed" (Tit. 2:4–5).

There are two points here: The first is that a woman's glory is her industrious fruitfulness flowing out of her home: serving the needs of her husband and children, showing hospitality, etc. And the second is that her husband's glory is to provide for and protect that fruitful home—to nourish and cherish his wife as Christ does the Church. And these are not interchangeable duties or responsibilities. To seek to reverse these roles is shameful. And it is particularly shameful for a man to play the part of a woman. It is shameful because it is an attack on the glory that God has established and assigned us in the world and for eternity.

Related to this is the duty of home defense and protection. The Bible says that it is an abomination for a man to wear the clothing of a woman, and it is an abomination for a woman to wear what pertains to a man (Deut. 22:5). Literally, the phrase could be rendered, a woman shall not wear the "gear of a warrior." While industrialization and technology really do effect what a woman *may* do and what a man *needs* to do, that fact must not be used to drive a relativistic wedge between this clear Word of God and a believer's glad obedience. And the issue is not primarily what a man or woman is capable of, but rather whether we are being obedient. A hammer is capable of stirring a pot of stew, but that is manifestly not what it's for. You might say that stirring a pot of stew is not the *glory* of a hammer. The glory of a hammer—what it was made for—is hitting nails.

The word for "abomination" means "confusion or perversion," and in the Bible it refers to the kind of activities that pollute or defile the land—homosexuality, bestiality, and idolatry, things that radically and willfully distort the order that God has established in the world and invite God's severe judgment (cf. Deut. 18:12, Mal. 2:11, Mk. 13:14). There is no need to make a legalistic list of things based on gender that a man or a woman cannot do. God has already listed specific things for us: a woman may not preach, for example (1 Tim. 2:12). And biology teaches us other things: a man may not become pregnant, no matter what the newspaper headlines say. But a love for God's law and natural law lead us to numerous other conclusions and norms that Christians must gladly embrace, embodying the glory of a man to provide for and protect his wife and children and home, and the glory of a woman to cultivate fruitfulness and beauty in her home. So female police officers and Marines and UFC fighters are abominations. The women who pursue such vocations are in sin, and the men who allow their daughters and wives and sisters to be seduced into such activities are even worse.

No, that doesn't mean a woman can't learn how to fire a gun or defend herself. Jael, wife of Heber, was plenty competent with a hammer and a nail when it was called for. And yes, sometimes there are hard providences where a man is incapacitated and a woman must provide for her husband, and in those cases, it is lawful and right that she do so. But exceptional situations do not make good rules, and hard providences hardly make ideals to aim for. Yes, Deborah was a godly judge in Israel, but it was shameful that Barak would not fight without her by his side in battle (Judg. 4:1–9). And all things being equal, it is an oppressive scourge when women and children rule over a nation (Is. 3:12), and not something we should be proud of at all, despite widespread "conservative" political acquiescence at precisely this point.

These are hard words, but they are *good* hard words. They are hard words for our good and blessing. And they are part of the good Word that husbands are commanded to wash their wives with. The image of *washing* indicates cleansing, purifying, and this is what God's Word does when received in faith and humility. It cleanses and purifies, and it does so by *clarifying*. It makes clear our discontent, our envy, our lust, our laziness, our selfish ambition in order that we can repent of it, and it simultaneously shows us what we are for, what men and women are clearly *for*, what a husband and a wife are *for*. And when we find out what we are for, we are being set free to live in the liberty of the Spirit—a liberty that will last into eternity. In other words, for a man to be faithful to his duty of washing his wife with the water of the Word, he must see to it that the Word of God is obeyed in his home, and he must see to it by leading the way in obedience and, where necessary, repentance.

Is it any wonder that in a day such as ours, when the light of the Church in the West has been reduced to such a faint flicker, these things must be said clearly out loud? Paul says that when he is talking about marriage, the calling of a man to love a woman faithfully, he is actually talking about Christ and the Church, but it really is a great mystery.

There's a sense in which Paul likely means this is really deep and profound and not easily understood. But there's likely another sense in which Paul is using the word "mystery." In fact, he uses the word in a number of other places in his letters, including several other places in Ephesians. And what becomes apparent is that the word "mystery" in Paul's use most often refers to something that was once hidden but has now been revealed: "Having made known unto us the mystery of his will ..." (Eph. 1:9). "How that

by revelation he made known unto me the mystery ..."
(Eph. 3:3). "Even the mystery which hath been hid from
ages and from generations, but now is made manifest to
his saints" (Col. 1:26). Even in Revelation, John hears
Jesus explain the "mystery" of the seven stars in His right
hand as the seven churches (Rev. 1:20). Therefore, while
there are no doubt depths of understanding that we have
yet to plumb, the primary sense in which Paul would have
us understand the "mystery" of marriage is the sense in
which it *reveals* and uncovers and proclaims the gospel of
Jesus Christ with clarity.

When Adam was cut open and Eve was created and
brought to him and the two became one flesh, that first
wedding was a "mystery" of the gospel—a picture of Jesus coming to save His bride. And then in weddings down
through the centuries that gospel meaning of marriage
was veiled and hidden to some extent, perhaps seeming
like a strange human curiosity, but again and again striking examples were woven into the text: Boaz and Ruth,
Hosea and Gomer, or the Song of Songs, repeatedly sug-
gesting that something else was at work: these marriages
seemed to be pointing to something to come. And then
Jesus came. He came as the great Bridegroom providing
the best wine at a wedding (Jn. 2). He came providing
food and shelter and healing. He came nourishing and
cherishing His people. And then He laid His life down for
His bride. He was struck in His side, and He died in her
place. He took her sins upon Himself to present her to
Himself "not having spot, or wrinkle, or any such thing;
but that it should be holy and without blemish."

In every wedding, in every marriage, God is saying, "this is a great mystery"—not as if we don't know the punchline. Every wedding, every marriage is a *revelation* of the gospel of Jesus and His Bride. It is the mystery that was hid in ages past but which is now made known to all men everywhere and will stand forever. This is what you are preparing to be as you are preparing for marriage. You are preparing to be yet another manifestation, another unveiling, another proclamation of the love of Christ for His Bride the Church. You do not have the option of opting out of this. You will do this whether you like it or not. Every marriage is talking about Jesus and His Church, either the marriage is telling the truth or else it is lying. Either the Word of Christ is dwelling richly in it or not. While this is terrifying in many ways, there really is great blessing in this, when we receive it by faith.

QUESTIONS FOR DISCUSSION

1. *What are your current Bible reading/prayer habits? Do you have any patterns together? If you're not married yet, what are your plans for when you get married?*

2. *What does "washing with water by the Word" mean, and what does it look like?*

3. *What is Church membership, and why is it important? How has it shaped your marriage or marriage plans to this point?*

4. *What does the man's responsibility to "nourish and cherish" mean practically for the roles of man and woman? How is embracing these roles part of being washed with the water of the word?*

5. *What does "mystery" often mean in the New Testament, and how will your marriage be a mystery of the gospel?*

CHAPTER 9

DEEPER MAGIC, DEEPER POWER

"LIKEWISE, ye wives, be in subjection to your own husbands; that, if any obey not the word, they also may without the word be won by the conversation of the wives" (1 Pet. 3:1).

The apostle Peter gives a number of instructions to Christians in his letter regarding how the gospel works itself out in all of life, beginning with prayer for kings and rulers, working through slaves and masters, and finally coming to this text for wives and husbands. These instructions are not merely good morals that make for decent, middle-class lives. These are instructions for people who will live forever. These are habits and patterns that are shaping believers into creatures of unimaginable glory.

What is so helpful about the examples that Peter uses is the fact that he reasons from very difficult circumstances, arguing *a fortiori* to what might be considered the more ordinary circumstances of life. *A fortiori* literally means "from the stronger," and in this case, Peter has just finished exhorting slaves to be subject to their masters, not only to the good and gentle but also to the difficult and abusive (1 Pet. 2:18–20). The point is that if the gospel pattern holds true in the most difficult circumstances, it most certainly applies in the normal day to day life.

This section of Peter's letter is what theologians and historians call a "household code," a collection of instructions for a household, found commonly in ancient literature. Paul's letter to Ephesus included a household code that we have already looked at in some detail, and Peter includes one here. The interesting thing is that in some ways the Christian household code echoes other ancient household codes, reflecting the natural law and common grace available to all, regarding the created order of man as the head of his household, a wife's submission and respect for her husband, and the obedience of children and so on. Nevertheless, unsurprisingly, the Christian gospel also subverts certain elements of the pagan household. But we need to be very clear here. Many modern exegetes want the gospel not merely to subvert certain elements of the pagan household, but also to overthrow the very concepts of household, hierarchy, and headship. But the gospel doesn't overthrow those things. Rightly understood, the gospel establishes all of those things, but it re-establishes them on the firm foundation of Christ rather than on the flimsy foundations of pride, various forms of vainglory and prejudice, and humanistic autonomy. But there are certain natural, universal practices, such as male leadership and responsibility, that remain intact, though revised according to the gospel. And to run back around the other side, this is not to say that paganism just got baptized. Jesus didn't come into this messed up world merely to put a Jesus fish tramp stamp on the back of whatever it was we were already doing.

No, what we were already doing from Adam's sin down to the cross and down to the present apart from God's intervention is a lot of oppression, tyranny, hatred, and violence. We needed to be saved from sin, death, and Satan, and so this is precisely why Jesus came. But despite our attempts to nuke everything, God's preventative grace did not allow us to destroy everything. God's natural law and common grace prevented us from completely demolishing everything. Gravity still exists. Male and female still exist. Basic mathematics still exists despite all of our best efforts to eradicate that as well. Turns out we still live in God's world.

So what do we mean then when we say that the New Testament reestablishes certain elements of the ancient household codes while subverting certain elements? In Ephesians, Paul does this by grounding male authority and headship in the cross of Jesus. The cross is the death of all sin, including all of the infamous male sins of pride, tyranny, abuse, ambition, and lust. The cross is also the death of all the infamous female sins like pride, manipulation, bitterness, vanity, and the lust to be desired. So whatever true and biblical male authority and headship are, they must flow from the cross of Jesus. And whatever true and biblical female submission and honor are, they must flow from the cross of Jesus. Peter does the same thing as Paul, but he takes the whole thing a step further. While Peter and Paul are in complete agreement, Peter makes the same point even more explicit by the *order* in which he addresses the members of the household. While Paul addresses the husband and wife first (perhaps somewhat subversively addressing them together, while affirming their differing roles and responsibilities), Peter *begins* with slaves, some of the lowest, weakest, and least respected members of a household who frequently have the least amount of power or protection or legal recourse.

If ancient household codes tended to focus on the responsibilities of the *paterfamilias*—addressing the head of the household, instructing him how to rule his household with dignity and equity, expecting him to address the various needs of his household—Peter begins by addressing the slaves. In effect, Peter assumes the powerless slave has, in some sense, one of the most powerful positions in the household by virtue of his powerlessness. This is not because the gospel immediately ended slavery, but because Jesus took on the form of a slave (Phil. 2:6–11). Peter points to the example of Jesus, who suffered unjustly, leaving us an example that we should walk in His steps (1 Pet. 2:21). Peter reviews the fact that Jesus did not curse at His abusers, did not revile when He was reviled, did not threaten those who struck Him, but instead He committed Himself to God who judges justly (1 Pet. 2:22–23). What did this accomplish? This accomplished the atonement for our sins: by doing this, God caused our sins to be laid on Him, that we might die to sins without actually dying the death they deserve—by His stripes we are healed (1 Pet. 2:24). The obedience of Jesus to the death accomplished our salvation, and even though we were like sheep all gone astray, Jesus brought us home by His suffering and death and resurrection (1 Pet. 2:25).

All of this is relevant to preparing for marriage because Peter is about to say, "Likewise, ye wives ..." (1 Pet. 3:1). Now it may not be very romantic to prepare for marriage by talking about disobedient husbands and suffering wives, and it certainly isn't very romantic. But it is manifestly *biblical*. In the one place where Peter gave instructions for Christian households, he addressed our needs using somewhat extreme examples. He argued from the extreme situations, so that we might know how to be faithful in the less extreme situations. And besides, Peter uses some wonderfully ambiguous language when he says, "If any obey not the word, they also may without a word be won ..." (1 Pet. 3:1). This is wonderfully ambiguous language because it could apply to really any husband anywhere. Even though it might most closely apply to an unbelieving husband or a radically disobedient husband, every wife will find herself married to a sinful husband, a man who at some point doesn't obey the Word. Hopefully, his heart is soft and the Spirit convicts him quickly and sin is confessed and forgiven quickly, but what should a Christian woman be thinking about in the five minutes or thirty minutes or six hours (or, unfortunately, sometimes longer) leading up to that confession and reconciliation? What should a Christian woman do when her man is in some measure disobedient? Peter addresses this by saying, "Likewise, ye wives ..."

Like what? Like slaves, like *Jesus*, "ye wives, be in subjection ..." Now clearly Peter has not taken any of our modern sensitivity training courses or political correctness seminars. Clearly, Peter is not "woke" or hip to the "social justice" reefer. And Christians must not merely be okay with this; Christians must be robustly enthusiastic about it. This is God's Word. It's glorious and good. It's gold, tested in the refining fires seven times. It's sweet honey. It's good milk. It's solid meat. And if Peter's language here makes you wince in the slightest, you really need to check yourself. Sure, people could get the wrong idea. God's Word can be twisted and misused, but God knew that when He inspired it, and Peter explicitly notes this possibility elsewhere (cf. 2 Pet. 3:16). But God understands words better than we do and certainly better than the modern politically correct grammar nannies. God understands the proclivities of sinful human hearts better than we do. And He inspired these words because He knew that we needed these particular words and not different ones. *These* words are inspired by God and useful to us just as much as all the soft and sweet passages (cf. 2 Tim. 3:16). But if we are willing to submit to God's wisdom even here, we will find that there are depths of sweetness for us here. Do you trust Him? Will you let God lead you? Will you be washed by the water of the Word?

So Peter says, "Likewise, ye wives," and yes, he is most certainly comparing the submission of a Christian wife to her husband to the submission of Jesus to His Father and the cross He suffered, as well as the submission of slaves who sometimes endured grievous and unjust suffering at the hands of wicked masters. This should not be understood in any way as a denigrating or demeaning comparison—just the opposite. First of all, it cannot be denigrating or demeaning because Jesus is at the center of it. It is always a deep honor to stand with our Savior. But let's not sidestep the fact that obedience to Christ will be seen as shameful in the eyes of the world. We go to Him "outside the camp" (Heb. 13:11–13), which is where the dump of Israel was. So yes, this may be offensive and appalling to modern minds, but this is part of embracing the shame of the cross. And yet, while there was true and deep humiliation in the cross, it was simultaneously Christ's great glory and the humiliation of all the principalities and powers (Col. 2:15). Furthermore, as Paul notes elsewhere, at no point did Jesus stop being God. He did not consider it robbery to be equal with God (Phil. 2:6). And although He freely gave up the outward glory of Godhead, He never for a moment demitted His deity. Therefore, if Christ, the God-man, can suffer injustice and shame and retain the dignity and glory of Godhead, a slave may suffer unjustly and retain his dignity and glory as a man created in the image of God, and a wife who suffers unjustly may likewise retain her dignity and glory as a woman created in the image of God.

Finally, nothing in this passage should be considered as pointers for mere *survival*. Christianity is not a religion for mere survivors. Christianity is a religion of resistance to sin, death, the devil, and all evil. Christianity is not a surviving religion; Christianity is a *conquering* religion. Christians, even those who suffer horrific injustice, do so in Christ, and therefore they are *more* than conquerors (Rom. 8:36–37). Therefore, Peter is not giving us or mistreated women pointers for survival. Peter has no interest in giving slaves and wives coping mechanisms until they get to Heaven. What Peter writes here is tactics for resistance, strategies for victory, the path of godly conquest. Our example is Jesus, who suffered and won. And here, Peter instructs wives how to *win* their disobedient husbands without a word.

Peter begins with the lowest members of the household, those with the least amount of apparent earthly power, and he works his way up through the household, ending with the husband and father, presumably the most powerful person in the household, the *paterfamilias*. In other words, he addresses the household in an apparently reversed order. By doing this, Peter is clearly not *upending* the natural order of the household, but he is upending the *sins* and misconceptions that tend to attach themselves to the natural order of the household. He is also challenging the humanistic assumptions that frequently accompany the exercise of power and strength in a fallen world. In our sinful state, people tend to embrace materialistic assumptions about power and authority: e.g., in order to make something move, you must make it move by superior force, by military might, by economic power, by brute strength, by violent revolution, by rhetorical prowess, by emotional or sexual manipulation, etc.

Even ancient paganism that believed in the supernatural realm of gods and demons rarely rose above a mechanistic view of the universe. Even if it was a god that caused a good harvest or victory in battle or marital fertility, it was the god that needed to be appeased, paid off, manipulated, or distracted with a sacrifice or offering or vow. It may have been mysterious and frustrating, but it still essentially reduced to a system of pulling this sacrificial lever to get this particular cosmic candy bar to drop into your lap, even if you occasionally had to shake the machine to get the candy bar to fall. So, according to the assumptions of fallen man, the slave has no hope against unjust treatment but to curse and fight back, the wife of a disobedient husband has no hope but verbal resistance and sexual manipulation to get what she wants, and the husband, if he sees trouble in the household, must rule with an iron fist, crushing all dissension through fear and bribes. But in reversing the order of instructions and in pointing to the example of Jesus, Peter points to a deeper order of power, a deeper sort of authority, or to quote Aslan, a deeper sort of magic.

The center of this deeper magic is the cross and suffering of Jesus and the justice of God. When Jesus was reviled, He did not revile in return. He was crucified for sins He didn't commit, but He did all of this for our sake, entrusting Himself to the One who judges justly (1 Pet. 2:23). And God used that apparent powerlessness as the potent explosion that destroyed the devil, crushed our sin, and is bringing all the lost sheep home (1 Pet. 2:24–25). Peter's point is that *this* is the center of Christian power. This is the deeper magic that God has embedded in the world. It's the power of pure blood freely shed for sinners. It's the power of pure justice served on a willing and innocent victim. But it isn't a mechanistic power at all. Nor is God tricked or manipulated. The power is the power of grace because this whole thing was God's plan. This is what Paul says elsewhere,

> For I determined not to know any thing among you, save Jesus Christ, and him crucified. And I was with you in weakness, and in fear, and in much trembling. And my speech and my preaching was not with enticing words of man's wisdom, but in demonstration of the Spirit and of power: that your faith should not stand in the wisdom of men, but in the power of God. Howbeit we speak wisdom among them that are perfect: yet not the wisdom of this world, nor of the princes of this world, that come to nought: but we speak the wisdom of God in a mystery, even the hidden wisdom, which God ordained before the world unto our glory: which none of the princes of this world knew: for had they known it, they would not have crucified the Lord of glory. (1 Cor. 2:2–8)

This *wisdom* of God is God's power or deeper magic. God's power causes all things to serve Him, all things to obey Him, and they do so not because He manipulates them but because He made them and understands them thoroughly and because they exist by the power of His

Word (Heb. 1:3). He need not coerce them, because they exist by His pleasure, by the overflow of His joy. They are His poetry, His songs, His artistry. All things delight to do His will. They exist in full harmony with their Maker. Of course sin and evil distort and twist this harmony, but evil is still parasitic off this fundamental harmony and goodness. Evil fundamentally turns back towards nothingness and non-existence. But all existence is goodness and glory because it proceeds from God Himself.

The point of all of this is that when Jesus entrusted Himself to His Father's justice, it was not apathy, not pacifism—no, it was the single greatest act of war on sin and evil. And so too all of those who entrust themselves to the Father by obedient faith in Jesus Christ find themselves *in* the powerful will of God, in the powerful justice of God, and therefore in the greatest position for resistance against all evil. Slaves and wives and husbands and all Christians are the most potent forces for good when they are most fully dependent on the God of the universe. And this is how a wife with a disobedient husband should have great hope of winning him over without a word. Whoever you are and whatever difficulty you face, the God of the universe offers you His power, His immortal power, when you entrust yourself to Him in obedience to His Word and the supernatural working of His Spirit.

QUESTIONS FOR DISCUSSION

1. *How is Peter's "household code" an* a fortiori *argument? Can you think of another* a fortiori *argument?*

2. *How do the biblical household codes affirm and subvert certain ancient assumptions about the household? Give examples.*

3. *Given the order that Peter goes in, what might be offensive to modern sensibilities about the phrase, "Likewise, ye wives ..."? Does this cause you any discomfort?*

4. *Why is Peter's phrase "if any obey not the word" wonderfully ambiguous? Who could that apply to?*

5. *What is the world's assumption of what power is? What does the gospel reveal is the deeper power/deeper magic at the heart of the universe?*

CHAPTER 10

HOW TO WIN A MAN

" LIKEWISE, ye wives, be in subjection to your own husbands; that, if any obey not the word, they also may without the word be won by the conversation of the wives; while they behold your chaste *conversation* coupled with fear" (1 Pet. 3:1–2, emphasis added).

It's perhaps worth remembering who wrote these words. It was Simon Peter, the fisherman turned lead apostle, the outspoken disciple, the one who confessed that Jesus was the Christ of God, the one who rebuked Jesus for saying He would suffer and die and rise again (and got rebuked for it), the one who cut off the ear of Malchus in the garden when Jesus was arrested, the one who denied even knowing who Jesus was before the cock crowed, and the one who was restored and commissioned to feed the sheep of Christ. Don't forget about the showdown with Paul in Antioch over Peter's hypocritical eating practices with Jews and Gentiles. And what I'm driving at here is that you ought not to forget that Peter was also *married* (1 Cor. 9:5). We know nearly nothing about her, but what a gem she must have been. Apart from Paul's passing reference in 1 Corinthians 9, the only other mention of Peter's wife is when Jesus healed her mother who was sick with a fever at the beginning of His ministry (Matt. 8:14).

The point is that Peter is likely not only speaking the truth about a wife's Christian duty toward her husband and how to win him to obedience to Christ, but he is likely speaking that truth from *experience*. We know so little about Peter's wife, but given what we know about *Peter* it would seem strange not to assume that his wife had played an important role in winning *him* at various points over the course of his life and ministry.

This language of "winning a man" also reminds me of the story of Jesus calling Peter to be His disciple in Luke 5. The telling of this episode is masterful. Luke describes Jesus beginning His itinerant ministry in Galilee at the end of Luke 4, then the next chapter picks up with Luke casually mentioning that Jesus found Himself preaching at the lake of Gennesaret and happened to see two fishing boats moored on the shore after a night of fishing (5:1–2). One of them turns out to be Simon's, and he pushes his ship out into the water and allows Jesus to preach on it for a while (v. 3). But then Jesus asks Simon to launch out into the deep and let his nets down. Simon reluctantly acquiesces to the request and soon finds his nets bursting. Even with the help of the second boat, they are both quickly on the verge of sinking (vv. 5–7). At this, Luke says, "When Simon Peter saw it, he fell down at Jesus' knees, saying, Depart from me; for I am a sinful man, O Lord ... And Jesus said unto Simon, Fear not; from henceforth thou shalt catch men" (vv. 8, 10).

There are a number of wonderful things about this story, but the one I want to highlight is how Luke describes Jesus *winning* Peter. Perhaps Peter initially thought Jesus was only interested in fish, but when the fish came pouring in, Peter realized that Jesus didn't really need fish. This is indicated by Peter's startling response to all the fish. The fisherman falls on his knees in shame, begging Jesus to leave because of his sin (v. 8). This is reminiscent of Isaiah's vision of the Lord high and lifted up. When Isaiah saw the Lord and the seraphim and the temple filled with smoke, he said, "Woe is me! for I am undone; because I am a man of unclean lips, and I dwell in the midst of a people of unclean lips ..." (Is. 6:5). Simon, like Isaiah, knows he is in the presence of a holy God, and he too is undone. But Jesus replies to Simon, "Fear not; from henceforth thou shalt catch men." Literally, Jesus says something like, from now on you will *catch men alive*. And the next verse says that the fishermen left their boats and nets and followed Jesus. But what this tells us is that Jesus did not go fishing to catch fish that day. Jesus went fishing with *Simon Peter* in order to catch Peter. Jesus caught Peter *alive*. Jesus *won* Peter.

No wife can be Jesus in this exact way, but every Christian wife is called upon to imitate the example of

Jesus. This is clearly the emphasis of the "likewise." Wives are to "likewise" be in subjection to their own husbands. Like what? *Like Christ.* And what is their aim? To be such examples of purity and holiness and fear of God that, if any husband is in disobedience to the Word of God, they might be *won* without a word, like how Jesus won Peter without a word.

This doesn't mean there isn't a word that needs to be said to disobedient husbands. There is a needed word, but it's a word straight from God. God knows what that needed word is far better than anyone else, including any longsuffering wife.

This is a general lesson for all Christians: sometimes we must be direct, speak the truth in love, and let the chips fall where they may, but other times we need to make sure we aren't getting in the way of what God is doing. God is sovereign, and He is not actually thwarted by any of our sloppy attempts at helping Him. But there is a great deal of wisdom to be learned in getting out of the way—leaving room for God to act, for God to deal with our situation, for God to speak the word that needs to be said. And this should never be an excuse for cowardice or laziness. If God drops the situation into your lap, then He clearly expects you to deal with it. But just because something is off doesn't mean it's your job to fix it.

This is a lesson for godly husbands as well: you are responsible before God for your wife, and you do need to lead her and teach her, but never forget that you are primarily commanded to wash her with the water of the Word—that is, God's Word. Sometimes there are things you must address directly with her right away, and sometimes the wisest course of action is for you to let God do the talking. Pray for her, read the Word to her, and get out of the way. Likewise, a Christian woman should want to win her husband without a word because she is eager to see God speak the Word for her, on her behalf. More on this as we continue to work through this passage.

This text is aimed directly at wives, but men should be taking notes. Here is a portion of the Word you are required by God to wash your wife with. You are responsible to lead and love your wife toward this obedient faith, an obedient faith that weathers storms, even (God forbid) storms of your making. You are tasked with winning your wife toward greater obedience to Christ, an obedience and wisdom that is unflappable, even when *you* are having a bad day.

The trouble, though, is *people*. Well, actually, the trouble is sinful people and angular people and petty people and fearful people and lustful people and ... did I miss anyone? And faced with the difficulties of people, the difficulties of *difficult* people, especially difficult *men*, the natural instinct of every son or daughter of Adam is to grasp for something stabilizing, something secure, something strong—some kind of power. Again, this is natural. When you're slipping or losing balance, you feel powerless, and, to be completely fair, you *are* powerless. And the less relative power you have, the greater the temptation to grasp for it. The deep irony is that all people are powerless. We are like ants swarming in a sidewalk crack, and a few of us think we're a little more safe because we have this thing called a 401K or a good job or a happy family. All of those things are great blessings, but they aren't secure. They are wonderful gifts that can be taken in a moment. Natural disasters, economic collapse, pandemics, war, famine, disease, and sudden death—we are all completely in God's hands at every second. It's all gift and none of it is secure.

This is your encouraging thought for the day. You're welcome.

But seriously, understanding the fleeting nature of life and our relative insecurity in this world really is the first step on the path to true security, true safety, and, actually, true power. And this isn't some kind of mind game. This is that deeper magic found in the cross of Jesus that we discussed in the last chapter.

Sinful human beings frequently grasp for alternative power sources rather than embracing the power that God Himself gives, the kind of power that *catches men alive*. There are sinful power-grab tendencies found in men and women, husbands and wives. In this passage, Peter addresses women tempted to use their words and beauty sinfully—to grasp for power, influence, security through them, and to give in to sinful fear, and he addresses each of these temptations in turn.

In the first instance, Peter urges Christian wives to seek to win over a disobedient husband *without a word*. Remember that this echoes the example of Jesus: "Who, when he was reviled, reviled not again; when he suffered, he threatened not; but committed himself to him that judgeth righteously" (1 Pet. 2:23). It was Christ's glory not to argue or threaten, but to commit Himself to God who sees all and judges all. If it was Christ's glory, it can certainly be our glory, even the glory of a woman whose husband is struggling to obey.

Solomon warned repeatedly about the temptation to try to fix problems with more words: "The contentions of a wife are a continual dripping" (Prov. 19:13). "A foolish woman is clamorous: she is simple, and knoweth nothing" (Prov. 9:13). "It is better to dwell in a corner of the housetop, than with a brawling woman in a wide house" (Prov. 21:9). "It is better to dwell in the wilderness, than with a contentious and an angry woman" (Prov. 21:19). "A continual dropping in a very rainy day and a contentious woman are alike" (Prov. 27:15). You might say this is something of a theme.

Wives, your verbal skills can be a great gift and a great help to a husband, but they can also do great harm. There are numerous other warnings about the tongue for all us. James says that the tongue is a flamethrower from Hell and sets whole worlds ablaze (Jas. 3:6). It's a wild, unruly beast that cannot be tamed (Jas. 3:7). The tongue is a sharp razor working lies, a sharp sword that stabs with bitterness, like the fangs of serpents full of poison (Ps. 52:2, 64:3, 140:3). What you may think of as "reminding" may actually be disrespectful nagging. What you may think of as "sharing" may actually be a "continual dripping on a very rainy day." What you may think is "getting advice" may actually be complaining, worrying, or worse.

Husbands must love their wives by teaching them the difference between helpful input and continual dripping, between respectful feedback and poisonous biting. This also requires husbands to have tight reins on their own tongues. A man who lashes out in anger or frustration at his bitter or angry or complaining wife is just throwing gasoline on the fire. A man who runs his mouth about his boss, his pastor, his parents, his kids, his elected officials is a man who is encouraging his wife and kids to do the same (and why not about him?). Sometimes a man may need to receive his wife's unhelpful words with grace and not respond immediately. He may need to pray about his own part in creating the situation or allowing a situation to develop where his wife is unprotected. But a godly woman should give heed to these warnings about her own tongue and not seek a fleshly power or security through her own words.

At the same time, there is a very important sense in which a Christian wife *must* speak to her husband. A Christian wife must bring her cares and concerns to her husband. One of the most common causes of marital bumps is the assumption that your spouse is a gifted telepathic mind reader. But let's be frank: while this can go both ways, the incidence is very high on the part of wives assuming their husbands know exactly what's going on and what's wrong right now. Let us also be frank about the other side of this equation: they frequently don't. The fact that you let out a sigh, glanced at the dishes, and said "Wow" several times would probably not register with the average guy.

Peter's point here is not an exhortation to absolute silence. He is not encouraging wives to assume their husbands will suddenly become psychics or mystically "figure it out." The point here is drawing a woman's attention to her God-given *power*. When something is not right, what do you think of as your power? Where do you think your strength is? Yes, you will likely need to use words in many situations, but do you think your words are your greatest power? If something is wrong, do you immediately think—I just need to explain it to him? *Maybe he didn't hear me the first time (or the first fifteen times!).* Peter says that your first recourse should be to live in submission to your husband with pure and godly conduct. This is actually basic Christian ethics applied to marriage. To change the context, how are you supposed to treat enemies? Christ says to love your enemy, to bless those who persecute you, and if your enemy is hungry to give him something to eat. If this is true of your actual enemies, how much more is this true if your fiancé or husband forgot to text you that he was going to be late for dinner? The answer is clear: you should seek to do him good. Keep dinner warm and cheerfully feed him when he finally arrives. You should think of that act of love and service in obedience to God as a means toward addressing any legitimate concerns—not in a carnal, manipulative way, but as an obedient, wordless appeal to God, your Judge who judges justly.

The key here is that this must be true virtue in the fear of God, and it must not be a pouting, fretting, or manipulative conduct. *Fine! Here's your stupid dinner* isn't exactly the spirit of Christ. Nor should your submission be an act of wheeling and dealing: *I'll give you what you want if you give me what I want.* If you're making the casserole while churning or scheming in your heart, you aren't making a "pure" casserole. It's a casserole full of sin.

The word in the King James for "chaste" means "pure" or "holy," and Peter says to let it be coupled with fear, meaning the fear of God. The only fear that is allowed for a Christian is the fear of God, "And fear not them which kill the body, but are not able to kill the soul: but rather fear him which is able to destroy both soul and body in hell" (Matt. 10:28). In fact, those who fear God cannot really fear man. "The LORD is on my side; I will not fear: what can man do unto me?" (Ps. 118:6) The fear of the Lord is the beginning of wisdom (Prov. 9:10), and wisdom recognizes that man is relatively nothing: his breath is in his nostrils (Is. 2:22). Therefore, a woman who knows her God and knows her identity in Him does not panic when her husband is late coming home from work (again), leaves the peanut butter jar out on the counter, leaves his socks on the floor, or gets irritated (or worse). She imitates her Savior, entrusts herself to "him that judgeth righteously," and puts on Christ to win her husband (back) to obedience. She seeks to submissively bless her husband in imitation of God whose goodness leads us to repentance (Rom. 2:4).

This is the source of all true power and strength: putting on Christ. Wives, submit to your husband in the goodness of Christ, in the purity of Christ. This is how you put on Christ. You put on Christ by faith, by fixing your eyes on Him, by trusting Him, and then *obeying* Him. In other words, you should go fishing. Make the casserole with joy. Think of something to say when he walks in the door that would be encouraging and gracious. Adorn your life, your home, your table, your bed, and, as we will see in the next chapter, even your body, with the goodness and purity of Christ. Let your conduct, your lifestyle, your "conversation," be full of the fruit of the Spirit because you fear the Lord and you do not fear any man, not even *your* man, who may not be obeying the Word at the moment.

Husbands, your responsibility is to teach and model for your wife *how* to do this. You do this in the first instance by making sure that you are in subjection to Christ. Many a husband complains (out loud or in his heart) that his wife is unsubmissive or disrespectful, and in that very act of complaining, he demonstrates at least one good reason why. How can you expect the one God has assigned to follow you to do any better than you? If you do not submit to Christ in your words or attitude about your wife, how can you expect her to do any differently? You *are* leading her, and she *is* following your example as you both complain right now. Therefore, this point of exhortation to wives is no excuse for a man to be lax or lazy before God. Instead, it is a call for men to be obedient to the Word and to be humble enough to be won back to obedience when necessary by their wife's chaste and submissive conduct. When you see your wife's pure and holy conduct, when you see your wife's nets full to the bursting with good gifts and blessing, it ought to inspire in you a similar response to the one Peter had when he saw the great haul of fish. It ought to remind you of the holiness of God and bring you to your knees. It ought to convict you of your sin. It ought to win you to Christ, and that very well might mean asking forgiveness for being late for dinner.

QUESTIONS FOR DISCUSSION

1. *Why is it interesting to speculate about Peter's wife when we read his words directed to Christian wives?*

2. *How did Jesus "win" Simon Peter? What does it mean to "catch men alive"? In what ways do Christian wives imitate Jesus in that?*

3. *When Peter urges wives to win over a disobedient husband "without a word," what does "without a word" mean (and not mean)?*

4. *Where is a woman's true power found? What are some of the ways you are both tempted to grasp for power? Talk through a situation where you might be tempted and what biblical power looks like for each of you.*

5. *What is a "pure" casserole? And how do you make one? What is a husband's responsibility toward his wife in this?*

CHAPTER 11

BIBLICAL BEAUTY

"WHOSE adorning let it not be that outward adorning of plaiting the hair, and of wearing of gold, or of putting on of apparel; but let it be the hidden man of the heart, in that which is not corruptible, even the ornament of a meek and quiet spirit, which is in the sight of God of great price" (1 Pet. 3:3–4).

Next, Peter turns to how a woman ought to think of the adorning of her own body. It is important to take these verses seriously, but it is also necessary to take them in context with the rest of the Bible. I was talking with an "egalitarian Christian" one time about Paul's prohibition of women preachers in 1 Timothy 2:12, and he insisted that if I took that prohibition of women preaching literally, I had to take 1 Timothy 2:9–10 literally:

"In like manner also, that women adorn themselves in modest apparel, with shamefacedness and sobriety; not with braided hair, or gold, or pearls, or costly array; but (which becometh women professing godliness) with good works." He was a little taken aback when I insisted that I do take that verse *literally*. But I explained that I take it literally according to the entirety of Scripture, or perhaps what might be better termed *naturally*, that is, according to its *natural* literal meaning.

For example, the Bible teaches that the glory of women is their physical *beauty*. Therefore, it is a godly and holy thing for women to submit to that assignment from God by adorning their bodies consistent with that. In marriage, part of that submission to God is manifest in a godly woman's submission to her husband in adorning herself *for him*. His tastes and preferences should be taken into account, and this means that men must love their wives by giving them helpful input and providing the means they need to be adorned graciously—this is part of his duty to nourish and cherish her. This is one of the ways that a man loves himself by loving his wife and quite literally presents her to himself adorned in beauty (Eph. 5:27). Part of how he does that is by giving her a clothing budget, occasionally taking her shopping, and telling her which dress he likes better.

The Bible teaches this at the creation of Eve, when the Hebrew says that God "made" the woman from Adam's rib—the word there is used elsewhere in Scripture for making pieces of art or sophisticated architecture. Likewise, when Adam says that the woman is "bone of my bones and flesh of my flesh," not only is this the first recorded love poem in the history of the human race, it is also an exuberant way of describing Eve's *beauty*. The Hebrew is a comparative construction—she is like man, only better, only *glorified*. This is what Paul says as well: "the woman is the glory of man" (1 Cor. 11:7), and this is why nature teaches us that women ought to have longer hair as their glory (1 Cor. 11:15). God created women to be physically beautiful. Embracing that assignment from God is true feminine submission to God.

Therefore, since God created the woman to be the glory of man, it is right and proper for her to embrace this by adorning herself *with* glory. This is why a bride has historically adorned herself with particular beauty for her wedding: "I will greatly rejoice in the LORD, my soul shall be joyful in my God; for he hath clothed me with the garments of salvation, he hath covered me with the robe of righteousness, as a bridegroom decketh himself with ornaments, and as a bride adorneth herself with her jewels" (Isa. 61:10). Here Isaiah says that when a bride wears a beautiful gown and glorious jewels she is picturing the glory of salvation. How beautiful is our salvation in Christ? It's like a glorious sunset, like rain coming down on mown grass, like a feast of fine wines and every good flavor. Likewise, John writes, "And I John saw the holy city, new Jerusalem, coming down from God out of heaven, prepared as a bride adorned for her husband" (Rev. 21:2). John will go on to describe the glory of the New Jerusalem, constructed with precious jewels and in architectural splendor. It is therefore good and right for a bride to proclaim the glory of salvation through her adornment, and if every wife continues to model the glory of the Church in her submission to her husband, then it is fully appropriate for her to proclaim that beauty with tasteful and beautiful makeup, hairstyling, clothing, and jewelry.

Therefore, we conclude that what Peter and Paul are prohibiting is flamboyant or ostentatious adornment, a haughtiness and pride that draws immodest attention to itself. The *literal* or *natural* sense of these exhortations is not a prohibition against beautiful dresses or jewelry or having your hair done. Otherwise, you are pitting God against Himself. If He is the one who clothes His own bride with beautiful garments and jewels, why would He prohibit husbands from imitating Him in that? He wouldn't, and He doesn't. But if you do not take the entire Bible into consideration when interpreting it, you will create numerous superficial contradictions that are based on unfaithful, simplistic interpretations. Do you really want to insist that Paul was disobeying Jesus when he said the Corinthians needed more "fathers" (compare 1 Cor. 4:15 with Matt. 23:9–10, which says "call no man your father upon the earth")?

Just as we noted that Peter is not prohibiting a woman from speaking to her husband about matters of concern when he says to seek to win him over "without a word," but rather is urging a Christian woman to remember where her power is, so too here, the same principle is at work. Peter is telling Christian wives not to think of their physical beauty, their sexual allure, as their primary power. Feminine beauty is a great and glorious gift from God, and it is part of a woman's calling from God. And when you read Song of Songs, you find that this adornment is a particular gift and blessing to her husband sexually.

However, just as a woman is tempted to use her words sinfully—clamoring, pestering, nagging, complaining, criticizing, tearing down—so too a woman is sometimes tempted to use her physical or sexual attractiveness to get what she wants. But Peter says that these natural gifts of beauty must always be subordinated to the deeper beauty, the incorruptible beauty hidden in the heart: a gentle and quiet spirit, which is most precious in the sight of God. So the question is: are you dressing that way because you know it pleases God and your husband? Or are you dressing that way hoping to get something? Are you trying to grasp for something, or are you offering a sacrifice of praise?

We could ask the same question in theological terms: Is your physical adornment justified? If you are a Christian, you are justified by faith alone in Christ alone. This means that God has declared you righteous, perfect in His sight only for the sake of Jesus. Your sins have been imputed (reckoned) to Him, and His righteousness and perfect obedience have been imputed to you. That is what justification means. So, is your clothing *justified*? Are your hair and makeup *justified*? What I mean is, has God accepted it? Is He pleased with it? Is it most precious and beautiful in the sight of God? This is the fundamental difference between adorning yourself to proclaim the beauty of salvation and adorning yourself with the insecurity of works-righteousness. Works-righteousness is trying to earn God's favor. It is trying to get God's attention, trying to be good enough. And this often happens through the attention of other people, popularity, or the opinions or glances of men.

We don't often think in crass terms about "earning" God's favor or blessing or salvation, but we do play mind games and substitute the favor or blessing of man for the favor or blessing of God. If people like us, we tell ourselves, we must be doing well. If we are getting a lot of positive attention, God must be pleased. But that is the adornment of insecurity and manipulation. That is grasping for power with the hand of human effort. It isn't God's way of power. That's a slick, addictive path that never actually delivers what it promises. It's a rat race, because you never know for sure if you've been good enough. You never know for sure if God is pleased with you. So there's always some doubt, some fear, some insecurity, which makes you an easy target for the next fad, the next fashion swing, the next marketing scam. A justified woman knows that she is *entirely* justified, inside and outside. If she is truly justified by Christ, then everything about her is justified. She stands completely secure under the infinite and indestructible pleasure of God. A justified woman is not trying to get God to like her. The glory of the gospel is that because of Christ, God already does. He rejoices over His blood-bought people with joy. He isn't *trying* to like us. He is already well-pleased with us. This verdict is what makes a woman's spirit quiet and gentle.

This is biblical beauty. It is the beauty of the gospel flowing from the inside out. It is the beauty of relief for sins forgiven. It is the beauty of grace—sheer kindness and abundant gift. This beauty is secure, confident, and glorious. It is an immortal beauty, a beauty that will last forever because it matches the goodness of God.

It should also be pointed out that there is more than one way to disobey this passage. One direction is straight up ostentation and immodesty, but sometimes a woman reveals her clamorous heart in the opposite direction. Maybe this seems impossible to imagine if you are newlyweds or still preparing for your wedding day, but you should never be surprised by the Twister moves of sin in our labyrinthine hearts. Sometimes when a wife is in a really bad spot, with an unbelieving husband or a disobedient believing husband, she can be tempted to "go on strike," so to speak. This may be in any number of departments, refusing to clean the house or prepare meals or keep up with laundry, overeating/undereating, refusing sex, and calling it quits on personal hygiene and presentation. Let's be clear: I'm not talking about a woman on bedrest not wearing makeup. Nor am I talking about having a home straight out of HGTV every day of the week. No, I'm talking about a persistent, perhaps even intentional sloppiness and apathy, sweatpants as the outfit *de jure*, and little thought taken for showing respect through thoughtful presentation for the man of the house. And if that sounds positively patriarchal, I assure you that it is.

Pretty sure that last paragraph is also illegal in several states. But I'm not sorry.

Sometimes this sloppiness is just ignorance. When this is the case, older women in the Church can come alongside a young bride and teach her how to keep a home and respect her husband (Tit. 2:4–5). But this is also something that husbands need to take responsibility for, even if it seems like something completely out of your range of expertise. It is your job to imitate Christ in your love for your bride. You are required by God to present your wife to yourself glorious, without spot or wrinkle, holy and without blemish (Eph. 5:27). A husband's love is designed by God to make a wife *lovely*—inside and out.

In order to address anything in this department, both husband and wife need to be committed to *biblical* standards for beauty. Besides being thoroughly disobedient, a man will make no progress in leading his wife if he is comparing her to the twinkies in bikinis on television. Likewise, a woman will make no progress in true feminine beauty if she is comparing herself (or being compared by her husband) to unrealistic and tacky fantasies rather than God's good and realistic word. And besides, it's thoroughly disobedient for a woman to get her beauty standards from our pornified culture. While there may be momentary thrills in mimicking the world's knockoff versions of sexy, the longer term results of allowing unbiblical beauty standards to creep into a Christian home will leave both husband and wife discontent, bitter, despairing, and apathetic.

Whether a wife is seeking to be obedient in her calling to adorn herself in the beauty of the gospel or a husband is considering bringing the topic up, the first step to addressing any of this should be honest prayer. Start by asking God to give you the ability to see and think clearly about these matters and be truly obedient to Him in them. Prayer should also be offered for any conversation, if there needs to be one. Then start with Scripture. This is the source of all our power and authority, for both husband and wife. What does the Bible say about what it means to be a man? What does the Bible say about what it means to be a woman? What is a husband? What is a wife? What are the respective glories of men and women according to the Bible? What does the Bible say about feminine beauty? Because Scripture is the Word of God, and because it is powerful and living and active, sharper than any two-edged sword, it is able to get at things that our fat thumbs often mess up. Frequently, in the course of prayerful Bible study, the topics that need addressing naturally arise, and practical conversations can begin. This is the gracious work of the Holy Spirit, and we should be sure to thank God when He does this.

We will get to this more in a later chapter, but a husband is required by God to understand his wife, and a wife is required to do her best to let him. Admittedly this is challenging task. Half the time, we humans hardly understand ourselves and our *own* thoughts and motives. Nevertheless, this is an assignment given to each husband by God, and so he needs to give effort to understanding why she does what she does and what she thinks about beauty and adornment, and from that place of understanding, he needs to lead her in love toward greater faithfulness. If there are tensions or frustrations in this area, is the root cause a biblical or theological issue? Does she understand what the Bible teaches? Is it a budgetary or financial issue? Is she concerned about spending too much money? Is it a taste or preference issue? Does she simply not know what you like? Is there some sin that needs dealing with? When's the last time you asked her if there was anything bothering her, anything she wants to talk with you about?

It also needs to be said that these questions and conversations need to be pursued with deep humility and heavy doses of good humor. If you can't laugh while having a conversation about clothing standards or the state of the home, you should probably spend more time in prayer and Bible study first. People are complex, and we often don't know why we think the way we do. The heart of a man or a woman is like deep water, and only a cheerful husband in spiritual scuba gear is likely to make much helpful progress. An overzealous husband with the attitude of a cross-examining lawyer is only going to make matters worse, especially after 10p.m. Relatedly: this pursuit of understanding is a lifelong mission. Ask any man who's been married for twenty or more years how well he understands his wife, and if he's honest, he will chuckle and say he's just scratching the surface—she is no mere mortal!

While Peter says that a wife's adornment must not be external, his point is that it must not be external in a way that is *inconsistent* with the internal, hidden person of the heart. The straightforward way for a woman to neglect Peter's exhortation is through cultivating bitterness and resentment in her heart, all while trying to dress up and keep a tidy home. In that scenario, a woman is acting the part of Pharisee, adorning the outside of her cup while allowing mold to grow on the inside. Inevitably, like all Pharisees, the outward result will eventually be immodesty, flamboyance, and ostentation. But the other way Peter's exhortation can be disobeyed is by letting mold grow on the inside *and* the outside of the cup. This will also result in immodesty and flamboyance, but it will be the ostentation of awkwardness for everyone around you and scared looks on the faces of small children.

You might wonder if it's possible to have a clean inside and grimy outside, and the answer is yes, but only temporarily, in the process of repentance. If you have to choose *today* whether you will confess your sins and get a clean *heart* or take a shower and tidy up the living room, pick confession of sin and a clean heart every day of the week. Better a clean heart and the joy of the Lord and whatever you threw on than a cute outfit and a heart full of fungus. Remember, "Better is a dinner of herbs where love is, than a stalled ox and hatred therewith" (Prov. 15:17). But truthfully, you rarely have to make this stark of a choice. Frequently, you can confess your sins, get a clean heart, and at least get a good jump on making that grace manifest. (Because, after all, that's what a clean house and hot meals are.)

One more thing really must be said about the center

of feminine beauty to which Peter calls women. He says it is a gentle and quiet spirit, which is most precious in the sight of God. First, simply note the contrast between the "gentle and quiet spirit" on the one hand and the "clamorous" and "brawling" and "contentious" woman Solomon warned about in Proverbs. The point here is not primarily about word count or average volume, though that is certainly something to monitor. The point is about peace count and joy volume. Is your heart at rest in God? In the midst of all the busyness of life, the meals, the carpooling, the logistics, paying the bills, the kids, or if you're in the middle of planning your wedding—is your heart full of peace and joy? Or it is clamorous and brawling and contentious? You may have the self-awareness and dignity to seal most of that up in your heart, but if you aren't offloading it to Christ and onloading His peace, the air pressure in there is going to reach maximum load very shortly, and something is going to blow. The blowup could be in anger—but it could also be a health meltdown, an anxiety attack, some kind of gluttonous or drunken binge, running your mouth about something you have no business sharing, or some other really poor decision.

But you might say, how do I do that? How do I juggle all these things without getting stressed and worried? Is that even possible? The answer is in the same verse and is related to what we noted earlier: a gentle and quiet spirit is *precious*—of great price—to God. That means you have a choice: either you try to be your own savior, your own god, and you try to juggle everything, which is another way of saying you will try to protect yourself or justify yourself ... or else you submit it all to God, surrender it all to Him.

Here's the thing: when you surrender it all to God, you are imitating Jesus, who "committed himself to him that judgeth righteously." What did God do with Jesus, who committed Himself to Him that judges righteously? God vindicated Jesus. God raised Jesus from the dead. God justified Jesus. God protected Jesus and proved Him right despite all the false accusations and the death sentence. This was because Jesus was *precious* to God. He was (and is) His *well-beloved* Son. The only person in the history of the world who could have had a shot at doing it all by Himself was Jesus: He was perfect. But even Jesus surrendered His will to His Father and trusted Him to protect Him and raise Him up. How much more so must all Christians, and Christian wives in particular, learn to do this?

What is your most valuable possession in this world? Think about it for a minute.

Okay, stop. Now, *where* is it? If it really is your most valuable possession, you know exactly where it is. You know where it is because you have put it there for safe keeping—it's in a strong box, a safe, in a special drawer, and it's safe and sound from all harm or loss. If you can't tell me where it is, I don't really believe it's your most valuable possession. Now, do you want to be in God's strongbox? Do you want to be in the safest place in all the world? Then cultivate a gentle and quiet spirit. The point of a gentle and quiet spirit is not apathy, not resignation to problems, and certainly not some kind of demeaning pat on the head. No, Peter is pointing you to the only place safe enough from all the storms, the only place strong enough to keep you from every danger, the only place of true security and Christian power. And really, if we've been paying attention, we need to realize that this power is nothing short of *resurrection* power—it's the power of God to raise the dead.

How do you practice resurrection? By dying. By dying to yourself, by dying to your dreams, your hopes, your expectations in obedience to Christ now, today. When you reckon yourself dead to the world, crucified with Christ, then God sees you in Christ and He does what He always does for Christ. He raises Him up. In other words, you can't make God raise the dead, but you can put yourself in the only place where God promises to raise the dead. You do that by reckoning yourself dead in Christ and then waiting for God's power to come. And it always comes. God's power always comes to those who wait on Him, to those who fix their eyes on Christ. It may not come in the way you might hope or expect, but it always comes.

So what are you practicing for now as you prepare for marriage or as you seek to be faithful in your marriage? Are you practicing resurrection power? Are you practicing true Christian feminine beauty? Are you taking your tips from the Bible and the example of other godly women, or are you studying *Glamour Magazine*, *Today's Bride*, and *Desperate Prairie Babes 3*? Or has any part of you decided not to care, not to even try? It's certainly true that charm is deceitful and beauty is fading, and that the fear of the Lord is the most lovely thing (Prov. 31:30). But the fear of the Lord doesn't just float up in the sky in some kind of airy-fairy way. The fear of the Lord is the beginning of wisdom, and Jesus is the wisdom of God *made flesh* for us and our salvation. Let your fear of the Lord be made flesh so that you will be afraid of nothing else. Since God is Lord of the whole universe, you can trust Him with everything. You cannot improve anything by worrying about it. This is true wisdom. Let this true wisdom be manifest in how you adorn your body, your home, your life, and do that by dying to yourself, dying to your sin, dying to your expectations and desires to control everything, and die so that God can raise you up. This is the source of all biblical beauty.

We will have plenty more to say to husbands and those preparing for the job in the coming chapters, but it's worth noting here, if briefly, that the beauty of salvation is something that is *bestowed* and *received*. This is what we mean by reckoning yourself dead and waiting for God to raise you up. Resurrection glory is only bestowed and received. When Lazarus was in the grave, he could do nothing to help Jesus. The beauty of salvation is like that for all of us. God gives it, and we merely receive it. While a Christian woman ought to be cultivating inner and outer beauty as her sacrifice of praise for the great salvation she has been granted in Christ—regardless of the obedience of the men in her life (husband or father)—it is nevertheless the great calling of fathers and husbands in particular to imitate this efficacious love of Christ. Just as Christ's love is efficacious in calling us out of the grave of sin and death and clothing all of us with the beauty of holiness, so too a man's Christ-like love for his bride is likewise efficacious. It isn't salvific like the love of Christ, but it is sanctifying. Over time, a well-loved woman really is more lovely, adorned like the bride of Christ.

QUESTIONS FOR DISCUSSION

1. *What is a literal interpretation of Peter's warning about jewelry and braided hair that takes the entire Bible into consideration? Why is it important to interpret it within this broader context?*

2. *What is the difference between a woman adorning herself with a gentle and quiet spirit and in the fear of God and a woman trying to use her beauty in a grasping or manipulative way? How is this connected to justification?*

3. *How should a husband or wife begin working through issues surrounding appearance and beauty? Why are humility and a good sense of humor important for these kinds of conversations?*

4. *What is a "gentle and quiet spirit" and how is it related to God's valuation of it as "precious"? Take turns discussing what this means. What are ways a husband can help his wife cultivate this?*

5. *What does it mean to "practice resurrection"? How do you do that practically when things aren't going the way you hoped or planned?*

CHAPTER 12

WHOSE DAUGHTERS
YOU ARE

"For after this manner in the old time the holy women also, who trust in God, adorned themselves, being in subjection unto their own husbands: even as Sara obeyed Abraham, calling him lord: whose daughters ye are, as long as ye do well, and are not afraid with any amazement" (1 Pet. 3:5–6).

As Peter concludes his instructions to women, he draws our attention to the "holy women of old" as examples of Christian adorning. And in particular, he points to Sarah. But it's worth asking: why Sarah? Of all the examples he might have chosen, why Sarah? Well, at the very least we can point to the fact that we have a fair bit of data on Sarah. We know that she followed her husband far away from her home and family and friends (Gen. 12:1–5). We know that Abraham asked her *twice* to identify herself as his sister and not his wife, and those situations got pretty sketchy (Gen. 12:13, 20:2). We know that Sarah had to endure her husband's nomadic lifestyle, the shame of barrenness, and the scandal of Hagar and Ishmael (Gen. 16). Perhaps the greatest horror of her life may have been the near sacrifice of her only son Isaac (Gen. 22). At the very least, we can see that Sarah did not have the easiest life in following her husband. We can also see perhaps why it was necessary for Sarah to "obey" her husband, calling him "lord" or "master."

The fact that even in conservative Christian "complementarian" circles this is the sort of verse that causes a great deal of squirming and throat-clearing is a terrible indictment of the modern "conservative" Church. It used to be common to hear the bride take a vow to "obey" her husband in the wedding ceremony, but to hear that sort of thing nowadays might get the cops called for a "hate crime" in some counties. But we really ought not balk at this kind of language. As we've noted previously, Christians (and non-Christians, for that matter) don't bat an eye at language that requires obedience to civil magistrates or police officers. But this tells you how lopsided our instincts have become. We have been trained, discipled, and—what's the word?—*conditioned* to have instinctive reverence for civil authority, but we are suspicious of familial or ecclesial authority. If the Bible commands us to obey our husbands or our pastors, we rush to the exceptions because of the potential abuses of authority. Lewis identified this tendency in *Screwtape Letters*: "The game is to have them all running about with fire extinguishers when there is a flood, and all crowding to that side of the boat which is already nearly gunwale under."[2]

If a police officer orders me to take a detour because of a car accident, I do not cry foul and flop like a soccer player, claiming to have been oppressed and repressed and hated and victimized and so on. No, I gladly *obey* the police officer because he's doing his job. And my *obedience* to the police officer implies nothing about my supposedly lesser dignity or inferiority as a human being. And the fact that many police officers have thoroughly *abused* their authority over the centuries does not even give me pause. Parents likewise have the authority to command their children *in the Lord*. And pastors must also require God's people to *obey* God's Word. This is not tyranny. This is not a statement about anyone's inherent value or dignity. It's merely the way God has ordered the world.

Husbands are responsible to lead and love their wives in submission to the Word of God (just like pastors and judges), and wives are required by God's word to *obey* their husbands *in the Lord* (just like congregants and citizens). When a military superior gives an order to a soldier, no one thinks the superior is gloating or degrading the soldier's inherent dignity. When a coach calls a play, the players do not protest the vestiges of the medieval patriarchy (usually!). This is the nature of the game, the nature of the world. The authority of pastors, judges,

---

2. *The Screwtape Letters* (New York: Macmillan, 1956), 129.

officers, policemen, and husbands is not absolute, but it is true authority granted by God.

When the husband and wife are both looking to Christ and His Word and are in good fellowship, many decisions by the husband will make sense to the wife because they are both reading the same playbook (the Bible). But as we've noted previously, there will sometimes be wisdom calls and decisions that need to be made (small and great), and when a Christian woman agrees to marry a particular man, she is promising to obey that man.

Remember too that this is not something that we are to grimace about as though we are slightly (or more than slightly) embarrassed by it. Not at all. The Bible teaches that this is a glorious picture of the gospel, the mystery of Christ and the Church revealed for the world to see. It is no insult to obey the Lord Jesus. It is our glory and honor to trust and obey, for there's no other way to be happy in Jesus. This is why I encourage Christian couples to include the word "obey" in the bride's wedding vows. Christians really need to stop apologizing for what the Bible says. Rather, we need to take what the Bible says and run it up the flagpole, celebrating God's Word and His instructions. Of course, this could be done in obnoxious ways, and I'm not condoning being needlessly belligerent, but there is strong biblical and historical precedent for a wife promising to obey her husband in the wedding ceremony—and besides, it's exactly what the Church does with Christ. And when your out of town relatives gawk at the "patriarchy," there you are with a wonderful opportunity to share the gospel.

Related to the obedience of a Christian bride to her husband is the title "lord." While I don't believe that Peter is requiring wives everywhere to use this particular title for their husbands, I do believe he is instructing Christian wives to speak to and about their husbands with deep reverence and respect. The casual and flippant ways that many professing Christian women speak to and about their husbands is a great stain on the testimony of the Christian church. When you're at the gym or the mom-and-tots playgroup is there a marked difference between how the Christian wives and non-Christian wives talk about their husbands? There *ought* to be. He's no mere mortal. He's an eternal soul, purchased by the blood of Christ, and indwelt by the Holy Spirit, and he is responsible for you. He will answer before the throne of God for his care and provision for you. All of this should make a Christian wife deeply joyful and deeply respectful.

You might not use the exact English term "lord," but think carefully about how you speak to and about him. I would also encourage you to avoid sarcasm and flippancy without becoming fussy or humorless. Aim for cheerful nobility, an exuberant reverence. Remember, just as loveliness is bestowed on you by his sacrificial love toward you, so too dignity, valor, and respectability are bestowed on him by your respect for him. While it may feel slightly awkward if you're not used to it, try saying, "Yes, sir," to your husband when he asks something of you. It may not be perfect, and perhaps there will be variations that fit your subculture better, but something like "sir" in modern American English captures something of the

natural respect a wife owes her husband without sound-
ing outlandish or making a spectacle of yourself.

The one historic record of Sarah calling Abraham
"lord" actually underlines this note of reverent joy. The
only recorded use of Sarah calling Abraham "lord" is
when God was talking to Abraham and promised that
when He returned within a year, Sarah would have given
birth to a son. The text says, "Therefore Sarah laughed
within herself, saying, after I am waxed old shall I have
pleasure, *my lord* being old also?" (Gen. 18:12, emphasis
mine). This hardly seems to be Sarah's shining moment as
a respectful wife, especially as she goes on to be confronted by God for laughing and she has the audacity to deny
it, even though God knows otherwise (Gen. 18:13–15).
But if we zoom out of the immediate context, we see that
Sarah's laughter in the tent is turned into a baby that is
named "laughter" ("Isaac" literally means "laughter"). I
take this to mean that Sarah quickly repented of her unbelief, and so she was genuinely happy to name her son (in
part) after her own doubtfulness and God's faithfulness.
In other words, God turned her fleshly, doubtful sarcasm
into a holy hilarity. It really was a great joke, really high-
born comedy, but the joke was on Sarah's unbelief. And
if all of that is true, then Sarah's address of Abraham was
also ultimately transformed. Her incredulous "my lord"
became a submissive and truly good humored "my lord"
in the act of sexual union that resulted in Isaac's conception, and ultimately it became a deeply respectful "my
lord" in bearing the promised seed for God's friend, Abraham, the father of all the faithful. All of this is a lesson

for modern Christian wives, tempted to be incredulous or flippant about their husbands, who are sometimes slow or difficult sinners, but who have nevertheless been filled with the Spirit of the King and granted true authority in marriage. May Christian women be known for their submission and respect for their husbands and always filled with an abiding and rollicking joy.

All of this is leads up to Peter's punchline, which really is quite striking: "whose daughters ye are" (1 Pet. 3:6). The biblical narrative is really clear: Sarah was barren for most of her life, and she was apparently only pregnant one time, and that one time was with her *son* Isaac. To point out the obvious, Sarah did not have any *daughters*. But Peter says that Sarah does have daughters. All those women who follow her example in adorning their lives with gentle and quiet spirits, those women who obey their husbands, are daughters of Sarah. And this is really wonderful if you think about it. This means that Sarah is an example of what God does with women who trust Him. A woman's gentle and quiet trust in God is precious, a most valuable treasure to Him. So what does God do? He protects His daughters. And Peter is pointing out that God is actually *still* protecting Sarah down to this very day. Sarah, the barren wife, is still being made fruitful to this day, and will be to the end of the world. Every woman who imitates Sarah's faith and submission is a testimony to God's sovereign care.

This ongoing *motherhood* of Sarah also establishes the fact that there is a very important sense in which all women are mothers according to the Bible. Biological motherhood is the central sign of this reality, but every woman participates in the calling of motherhood by her imitation of Sarah's *faith*. Is Sarah the mother of faithful women? Then you too are a *mother* as you walk by faith and make the world around you fruitful and lovely. The Bible repeatedly testifies to this reality: Deborah was a mother in Israel through her political ministry (Judg. 5:7). King Lemuel's mother is enshrined in Proverbs as a mother of all young men seeking wisdom and an excellent wife (Prov. 31:1ff). Paul asks the Romans to greet a man named Rufus and specifically his mother, who had been a mother to him as well (Rom. 16:13). And the Christian Church is the Mother of us all (Gal. 4:26). Motherhood is faithful fruitfulness. Christian motherhood instructs, comforts, conceives, nurtures, and cultivates life and beauty. None of this is to take away from the glory of biological conception and motherhood, but just as inner beauty is designed by God to manifest in various forms of outer beauty, so too this faith-filled motherhood manifests in various expressions of fruitfulness, and ordinarily in the physical bearing of biological children—but fruitfulness is not limited to that.

All of this is also related to what Paul says elsewhere in a somewhat challenging text: "Yet she will be saved through childbearing—if they continue in faith and love and holiness, with self-control" (1 Tim. 2:15, ESV). It's striking that in an apparently *liturgical* context, Paul points to the unique calling of women to be child-bearers. One minute he's talking about men raising hands in prayer and instructing women not to teach and have authority over men, and the next he's referring to women bearing children. It might also seem a bit odd since Paul is here speaking about men and women more generally, not explicitly about husbands and wives and marriage. But Paul's logic actually makes sense if we think of the creational context of Genesis. The garden was the original sanctuary, where Adam and Eve met with God and communed with Him. And it was in that sanctuary where the first man and woman were created that the first sin occurred. And there, in that first sanctuary, God proclaimed that the solution to sin would come through the "seed of the woman," and Adam named his wife "Eve" in faith and repentance, believing that she would become the "mother of all the living" (Gen. 3:20).

This makes sense of how Paul would think of childbearing in the context of ordering a Christian worship service rightly. Paul does not mean that a woman will be saved through childbearing in a crass, materialistic way. He isn't saying that bearing children takes away sin, or that a mother with six children is more godly than a mother with two children. Rather, he is saying that together with faith, love, holiness, and self-control, motherhood is part of God's plan of salvation for the world (e.g., Ps. 8, 127). A woman, embracing her calling to faithful fruitfulness (motherhood), is not a second-class citizen in the worship assembly. She may not teach or have authority over men, but precisely *as a mother* she plays a powerful role in God's great war on sin. The central fulfillment of that promise was in the birth of Jesus to Mary—we are all saved through *that* childbearing. But I take Paul to be saying that there is still a general pattern here to be followed by all believing women. Or to put it another way, there is a feminine-shaped faith, love, holiness, and self-control that is uniquely maternal and fruitful and used by God to bring His salvation to the world.

One final note here is that Peter says that a woman who submits to her husband is a daughter of Sarah if she is not afraid with any terror (1 Pet. 3:6). Just as women are often tempted to take matters into their own hands by their words or their beauty, another common temptation for women is fear and anxiety. So this is the final thing that Peter urges Christian women to adorn themselves with: peace. A gentle and quiet spirit cannot be full of turmoil and tumult. If God is still protecting Sarah, still blessing Sarah by making her a fruitful mother of believing women down to this day, thousands of years later, God can be trusted to handle whatever you may face. If God can continue making Sarah fruitful long after Sarah is in the grave, then He will protect you whatever comes your way. You have nothing to fear.

QUESTIONS FOR DISCUSSION

1. What are some reasons Peter may have had for using Sarah as his example of women of old to point Christian wives to?

2. Why should Christian couples consider including the traditional vow for the wife to "obey" her husband? What do our aversions to that word indicate?

3. How do Christian wives apply Sarah's example of calling Abraham "lord"? What's striking about the context of the only recorded instance of Sarah calling Abraham "lord"?

4. What is significant about the promise that women who follow Sarah's example become Sarah's daughters/children? How does this prove that all Christian women are called to some form of "motherhood"?

5. How does God's blessing of Sarah (down to the present day) give a Christian wife deep peace and the ability to trust God and fight anxiety and fear?

CHAPTER 13

DWELLING WITH
KNOWLEDGE

"LIKEWISE, ye husbands, dwell with them according to knowledge, giving honour unto the wife, as unto the weaker vessel, and as being heirs together of the grace of life; that your prayers be not hindered" (1 Pet. 3:7).

After all that Peter has covered with servants and wives, it may seem a little strange that Peter spends relatively less time and space on instructions for men. This is because Peter knows that men have short attention spans.

Actually, it's more likely that Peter knows that men generally do best with direct, blunt instruction. But regardless, we should not miss the fact that Peter once again says "likewise." In other words, part of Peter's point is that many of the same principles that have already been covered apply to husbands as well. In the word "like-wise," Peter is instructing husbands to do the math, make the appropriate translation of the previous principles to the station and calling of "husband," with the additional instructions listed here. So I hope you all were paying attention in the chapters addressed to your wives.

The other thing that should not be missed is that the "likewise" means that there is a sense in which a husband is required by God to follow the example of His wife in following Christ. This goes way back to where we began, grounding our identities in Christ. If a woman is in Christ, she is a new creature, and she is a glorious image and representation of Christ. A godly husband must see that and follow his wife's godly example as she follows Christ. She is an immortal, in the process of becoming a creature you would one day be tempted to worship. This is one of the implications of Peter's order-reversal in this household code. A woman follows the example of a servant, who follows the example of Christ. And therefore, a man is to *likewise* follow the example of his godly wife, who is following the example of believing slaves (also immortals), who are following the example of Christ. This is further underlined by the fact that Peter has just finished exhorting wives to adorn their lives with such gospel beauty that they win over any husband who is not being obedient to the Word. The whole idea is to win a husband over to obedience, and even if your husband (or husband-to-be) is not in any high-handed disobedience, your gospel adornment should be in part calculated to encourage your husband in godliness, to cause him to want to seek Christ more, or *likewise*.

The first specific instruction to husbands is to dwell with their wives with understanding, or according to knowledge. In order to obey this command from the Lord you must actually *dwell* with your wife: you must live with her. And this means that you must be home sometimes. Now, don't misunderstand: A man is required by God to provide for his family, and this will require you in most scenarios to be away from home for stretches of time. But then you must come home. For most men this will mean coming home at the end of the day, for some this will mean coming home after deployment or after the business trip, and maybe for some it will meaning coming *into* the home after a day out in the fields, or coming *out* of the home-office to be home. But in the ordinary course of things, a husband must regularly make time to *dwell* with his wife. He must be *present*. But it is not enough to be located at the same address, to be merely breathing in the same space. Peter says that a husband must dwell with his wife *with understanding*. You need to be around your wife with awareness; you need to be home *with the lights on*, taking careful notes.

You are embarking on a post-graduate course, a life-long study of your wife, an immortal, made in the image of the infinite God. Good luck! There's more than enough material there for a single lifetime even if she never changes, but the really fun part is that your wife will grow and mature over the course of her life. Some of this will simply be changes in preference and personality, but some of it will also be the result of her growing up in maturity and wisdom in Christ. And remember, this is part of what you are signing up for. You are to love your wife as Christ loved the Church and gave Himself for her, "that he might sanctify and cleanse it with the washing of water by the word, that he might present it to himself a glorious church, not having spot, or wrinkle, or any such thing; but that it should be holy and without blemish" (Eph. 5:26–27). You have to dwell with your wife according to knowledge so that you can love her well.

Men, this means that you must ask lots of questions. We've covered a number of the temptations of women in recent chapters, but one of the central temptations of men is pride, and this is directly related to why men don't like asking for directions or reading instruction manuals. Men want to be smart, intelligent, and want praise and kudos for their accomplishments. Now, there really is something glorious about this independent instinct. It gets mixed up with sin and the flesh, but the instinct is actually good and holy and masculine. It's the instinct to take responsibility, to serve, to be useful, and even though it can be taken to extremes, the survivalist in every man wants to test his ability to figure out problems on his own. There is real glory in that. But, men, here you have God Himself telling you that you don't know how to love a woman well, and you certainly don't know how to love *this* woman like you need to. There is no YouTube DIY video for this (I checked).

Marriage is one of God's great jokes on the human race. Don't get me wrong: it's a wonderful joke, a really good joke, but it's still funny. And there are several levels to the humor. First, just note that the second greatest commandment is to love your neighbor as yourself. And then remember that people are really different. So loving your neighbor as yourself is a great *start* at learning to love other people and learning to love a wife well. But it's just a start, because five minutes after you begin, you'll realize that even though you love watching football or war movies or drinking dark beer, your wife may have somewhat different preferences.

A number of years ago, I purchased the book *The Five Love Languages*. To put it mildly, this book is not at all the sort of thing I'm drawn toward, but given its popularity, I decided that I should at least have a cursory understanding of what I thought I didn't like. I was mostly confirmed in my suspicions and haven't picked up the book since. (Guys, you can thank me for taking one for the team. Keep reading closely so you don't ever have to bother with it.)

The whole thing is loosely based on a very common-sensical idea: *people are different*. Anyway, at the back of the book is a quiz you can take to find out what your "love language" is, and I decided it would be fun to take my wife out on a date and take the quiz together. Now you have to understand that by this point, we had known each other for over fourteen years. We had met as freshmen in high school and married halfway through college, and by the time I took her out on this Love Language Date, we had been married for well over eight years. But the date was hilarious. It was hilarious because we had a number of great laughs over things we thought the other person liked that, turns out, were not exactly their favorite. Some of those things were things we used to like, but our tastes had changed, and some of them were just things we hadn't ever really picked up on. Anyway, all that to say, loving another person means learning about them, studying them, asking questions, maybe even taking notes, writing down ideas and reminders, taking a silly quiz, whatever it takes.

Now understanding a woman also includes understanding her weaknesses, her temptations, and her proclivities to sin. The danger of some of the "love language" business (along with many of the personality test fads) is that people can use those categories as excuses for sin. For example, instead of repenting of your rudeness, you just excuse yourself because you're introverted or extroverted as you rattle off several letters or numbers that supposedly describe your personality—as though that's a legitimate excuse for your sin. But there are no excuses for sin. That's why we need to be forgiven and why we must *repent*. Just because we are drawn to particular kinds of sin doesn't mean we're free to keep sinning that way. Just because we have certain bad habits or tendencies from our parents or our upbringing or our bodies doesn't mean we are free to go on sinning in those ways—even if it really is in your blood or genes! According to the Bible, Adam's sin really has been passed down through generations. We may not understand all of the ways we are tempted or inclined to sin, but if it is sin, it must be mortified, put to death, repented of, *daily*. If we are sinfully blunt or sinfully shy or sinfully disorganized or sinfully forgetful or late or chatty or lustful, we must confess our sins, repent, and put on Christ. A husband has the sacred duty of understanding his wife so that he can help her put on Christ. And, wives, if you have agreed to marry this man, then you have agreed to let this man help you with your weaknesses. This is part of his assignment from God, and you really ought to work hard to make that task a blessing and not a hardship (cf. Heb. 13:17).

The other half of the joke of marriage is that not only are people different, but that, in the mosh pit of different personalities and preferences and strengths and weaknesses, God threw the knuckleball of different sexes: male and female. You know God was chuckling when He did that. *Now this will be entertaining.* A few of the angels no doubt wondered whether it was such a good idea.

There are various levels to their differences, but consider the way men and women tend to relate, for starters. I think it's C.S. Lewis who said that men tend to be friends shoulder to shoulder, facing a common mission or project or problem. Men stand side by side as comrades, teammates, co-workers. Male friendship tends to focus on accomplishing a mission together, overcoming a problem together, and celebrating and remembering those victories and accomplishments together. On the other hand, Lewis noted that women tend to experience friendship face to face, relating more directly to one another, sharing their stories, their thoughts, their feelings on various tasks, concerns, and challenges.

Another general difference between men and women is the fact that men tend to assume everything is fine unless it obviously isn't. Ask some guy how his friendship is with Joe-Friend, and he's likely to consider everything great if he hasn't gotten into some kind of fistfight or argument recently with Joe. They may not have talked or texted or seen one another for years, but if nothing has interrupted the friendship, all is generally assumed to be well. On the other hand, women tend to relate to one another in far more affirming ways, and if they haven't heard from someone recently, they might wonder if everything is still good. These generalizations have any number of exceptions or nuances, but you get the idea. And God thought it was a great idea to throw us together into the covenant of marriage.

A man understanding his woman means that he needs to understand that she will generally expect far more affirmation than he will ever need for himself. A man might be tempted to tell his wife something like, "I said I love you on our wedding day, and I'll let you know if anything changes." (By the way, just my two cents, but I would suggest you *not* say that.) A man needs to remember that God specifically commanded him to *love* his wife as Christ loved the Church (Eph. 5:25). This love includes nourishing and cherishing your wife, literally, as we noted previously, *feeding and keeping warm*, and we can confidently say that these are *ongoing* duties of a husband. It's not enough to buy groceries or take your wife out for dinner one time. This is an ongoing duty, and so you need to tell your wife that you love her and that she is beautiful *regularly*. And you need to do this for the same reason you need to buy groceries and take her out for dinner regularly: telling her that you love her and that she is beautiful is *food* for her soul. This is generally borne out by human experience, but if you were in any doubt, we know that God feeds His people by His Word. Man does not live by bread alone, but by every word that proceeds from the mouth of God. If God nourishes and cherishes His people with His Word regularly, so too a husband must nourish and cherish his wife through his words regularly. And though it may go without saying, let your words be full of kindness, blessing, gratitude, and praise.

While we are here, the converse exhortation can be given to wives and women preparing for marriage: Remember that your husband or fiancé is a man. And just to make this clear, this means he is not a woman. Remember that he is not like you, and while he most certainly must dwell with you in an understanding way, this is not some kind of blank check for you to be demanding, manipulative, or difficult. You also need to dwell with him in an understanding way. Let your man be a man. Let him go to work. Let him give himself to his work. Don't just *let* him somewhat begrudgingly. Cheer him on in his work, encourage him as he tackles various projects, and welcome him home warmly. Let him know that you support him in his mission, that you respect him for his decisions and responsibilities, and make his job of leading you and living with you a delight. You're on his team. Of course you may let him know if there are ways he can love you better, but remember that there may be some things that you *think* you need that your husband, after prayer and consideration, may decide that you don't need. He may or may not be right about that decision, but you are called by God to submit to him joyfully.

One more point on dwelling with your wife according to knowledge, but first a qualification: I wouldn't go to the stake over this next point in terms of exegesis. I'm not sure if Peter had this in mind or not or if the Holy Spirit did. But even if this is a bit of holy free-association, I think it's certainly consistent with the overall teaching of Scripture. The language of a man "knowing" his wife is reminiscent of the Old Testament euphemism for sexual intercourse: "Now Adam *knew* Eve his wife, and she conceived and bore Cain" (Gen. 4:1, ESV, emphasis mine, cf. 4:25). Again: "And Cain *knew* his wife, and she conceived and bore Enoch. And he built a city" (Gen. 4:17, emphasis mine). And much later: "And Elkanah knew Hannah his wife, and the LORD remembered her. So it came to pass in the process of time that Hannah conceived and bore a son" (1 Sam. 1:19–20, NKJV).

My point is that a man being commanded to "dwell with them according to knowledge" at least reminds me of the fact that a husband is commanded by God to diligently pursue his wife *sexually*. A man must *know* his wife in this sense as much as any other sense. All things being equal, God generally gives a much stronger sex drive to men, and that is a gift for marriage. Men, let your drive to *know* your wife in the marriage bed be a metaphor for how you search her out in every other area. Women, let your husband's pursuit of you in bed be a metaphor *to you* of how he is to pursue you with understanding in all of life. Warmly welcoming him there is a warm welcome to him everywhere else. This is an *honorable* thing. The marriage bed is to be honorable among all men (Heb. 13:4). A man is to be intoxicated by his wife continually, and her breasts are to satisfy him at all times (Prov. 5:19). The command to nourish and cherish your wife also includes the nourishment and cherishing of sexual intimacy (Eph. 5:29).

But all the same principles apply here as much as anywhere else. A man must be a student of his wife sexually. One of the great lies of modern pop culture is that sex is always and immediately really easy and fun. Despite all of your necessary and valiant attempts at avoiding modern media on the subject, you will have no doubt noticed that everybody going about their sexual escapades is pretty much always having an awesome time. Now of course, God created sex. It was His idea. It is a really good thing. Sexual intimacy in the context of the covenant of marriage is blessed by God, and so it is an entirely natural, right, and holy good time (see Song of Songs). But like everything else in marriage, it does take some work and practice. You may enjoy dancing, but the first time you tried dancing, you probably had to learn a few steps. Most really good things in life take some effort to learn how to do them well. So too, making love. And men, you are specifically required by God to study your wife *here.* You need to dwell with your wife in the kitchen in an understanding way. You need to dwell with your wife in the living room in an understanding way. You need to dwell with your wife in the bedroom in an understanding way. You need to ask questions, talk openly and honestly about any challenges or difficulties or frustrations, and you need to keep working at loving your wife well *here*. If you go into marriage believing the lies of the world, that it's all easy sexual ecstasy from your wedding night until you pass over into heavenly glory, I submit that you will face certain frustration and disappointment. You will also be a really lousy lover.

Of particular note on this subject is the general truth that, when it comes to sexual appetites, men are like microwaves and women are like crockpots. Men tend to be far more visually stimulated, and because God made men to be initiators, they tend to have more of a sexual appetite. This is not always true, but it often is. So, applying Peter's instruction here, men must understand that their wives will generally need quite a bit more pursuit and romancing. This includes how you talk to her throughout the day, helping with the dishes, praying with her, playing with the kids, compliments for dinner, and occasionally pulling her aside and giving her a good kiss. This is by God's design. God saw all that He had made, and it was very good (Gen. 1:31). It is good for a man to pursue his woman, and it is good for a woman to be pursued by her man. Remember that. But remember that this is often a source of temptation and sin. Because men are generally plagued with temptation to laziness, a fair bit of frustration and resentment stems from men wanting easy sex and women wanting men to spend more time pursuing them. A woman's sex drive is more complicated than a man's, generally fluctuating with her menstrual cycle, and while her short-term sexual needs should be met, one wise man has noted that a woman doesn't fully climax until a child leaves the home and gets married. A man needs to understand all of this about his wife and learn to meet her needs, but this also means that it is his responsibility to teach his wife how she may meet his needs. God made these different tendencies, and they need not be at odds.

On this topic, Paul says that married couples should have sex regularly (1 Cor. 7:3). It is a sin for one spouse to deprive the other of sexual intimacy except by consent and only for an agreed upon time for fasting and prayer (1 Cor. 7:5). There are not that many explicit warnings about Satan in the Bible, but this is one place where the Bible explicitly warns married couples not to mess around. Or rather, they do need to regularly mess around in the marriage bed so that Satan does not weasel his way into their marriage through sexual temptation (1 Cor. 7:5). While it is certainly true that both men and women can be tempted sexually, it is often the case the men are more vulnerable, and therefore Christian wives really do need to understand how they can be significant helps to their husband in his battle for purity. But again, here Peter says that it is the man's job to dwell with his wife in an understanding way. This means you need to understand what your wife thinks about sex, what she thinks about your sex drive, what she thinks about sexual temptations, what her sexual needs or concerns are, etc. A faithful and godly husband comes to understand these things and discusses them with his wife, making sure that she has a *biblical* understanding of these things and knows how she can be his friend and how he can be hers. A helpful resource on this topic is a short booklet called *False Messages* by Aileen Challies.[3] Aileen writes to Christian wives, seeking to help them understand male sexual temptation and how to respond biblically.

Related to all of this would be my recommendation that couples get and read a book like *Intended for Pleasure* by Ed Wheat.[4] I generally encourage engaged couples to take turns reading it in the weeks leading up to the wedding, and then maybe a week or so before the wedding have a conversation about it. *Intended for Pleasure* will also be a helpful resource and encouragement for married couples to revisit occasionally over the years. The conversation need not be overly graphic or lurid before the wedding, but it can cover any concerns or questions that need addressing before the wedding night. Of course couples must remain pure all the way up to the wedding day, but it's not impure to make some preparation for what everyone knows is coming. Christian parents and family members can be very good resources in this regard as well. Otherwise, Christian couples are left to their own imaginations or fears or Google roulette.

---

3. Available for free download at https://www.challies.com/sites/all/files/attachments/false-messages.epub.
4. Grand Rapids, MI: Revell, 1997; 4th ed., 2010.

QUESTIONS FOR DISCUSSION

1. *What does Peter's "likewise" mean for husbands in 1 Peter 3:7?*

2. *What does it mean that a husband must dwell with his wife with understanding?*

3. *What are some of the common differences between men and women? How do those differences play out in your relationship with your fiancé/fiancée or spouse?*

4. *Why can the duty of "dwelling with knowledge" include sexual intimacy?*

5. *How is regular sexual relations part of spiritual warfare according to 1 Corinthians 7?*

CHAPTER 14

STRENGTH TO HONOR THE WEAKER VESSEL

Peter's next exhortation to husbands is that they must honor their wives as the weaker vessel. Despite all the modern attempts to explain this verse away, Christians must simply embrace this verse without flinching in the slightest. Here it is clearly: Christians believe that God created women in His image, and they are generally weaker than men. Let the five minutes of hate begin.

But we can and should say more. Remember the Chesterton poem "Comparisons" that I alluded to in an earlier chapter:

If I set the sun beside the moon,
And if I set the land beside the sea,

And if I set the flower beside the fruit,

And if I set the town beside the country,

And if I set the man beside the woman,

I suppose some fool would talk

About one being better.

To say that something is weaker than something else is not a statement about its inherent value or dignity. A pocketknife is weaker than a chainsaw. But a pocketknife is far better for some things than a chainsaw. A woman is better at making babies than a man. In fact, just to be clear in these confused and confusing times, men can't even make babies inside of themselves at all.

So what does Peter mean by "weaker vessel"? Well, the biological fact is that men are generally physically stronger, and this is generally credited to the higher testosterone levels naturally produced by the male body. Yes, I know that there are some women out there who are stronger than some men. Very good. But the glory of men is their strength (Prov. 20:29; 1 Jn. 2:14). When Paul urged the entire church of Corinth to be strong, he exhorted them to "act like *men*" and be *strong* (1 Cor. 16:13, emphasis added). In the Old Testament, when men and nations are overcome with fear, especially in battle, they are likened to women (Is. 19:16; Jer. 50:37, 51:30).

Related to the biblical requirement that men be strong is the requirement that Christian men not be *soft*. Soft men do not and cannot honor the relative weakness of their wives well. This honor that God requires of men is an honor laced with masculine strength. This is a teaching that has become almost entirely absent from the modern evangelical Church. The great virtue of the modern evangelical Church is "niceness," which we should note is not actually one of the fruits of the Spirit. What we are arguing for here is not pseudo-masculine Rambo dudes. We are not arguing for WWE-wrestling-style Christianity. But be assured that a man who takes his responsibility seriously to be strong will likely be accused of it anyway.

So what am I saying? I'm saying that every man has been given the assignment to cultivate strength in order to sacrificially love and protect those around him. A man need not be a heavyweight or a black belt, but he must cultivate strength. This strength includes spiritual and emotional fortitude, which is the ability to cast his cares on God so that he doesn't dump his feelings on his wife and kids. This is the strength of stability: getting up and going to work every day, coming home after work every day, being joyful and encouraging every day, being a rock of moral conviction every day. This is biblical and masculine strength.

The opposite of this strength is effeminacy or softness. 1 Corinthians 6:9 says that the *malakoi*, the soft, will not inherit the kingdom of Heaven. In that context, Paul is clearly associating it with homosexual sin. Robert Gagnon has shown persuasively that this word should be understood both in this explicitly sexual way and in various other ways a man might feminize his appearance or manners.[5] This may be in overtly "metrosexual" ways or in acceptably "Christian" ways. We see this in the way the

5. Robert A.J. Gagnon, *The Bible and Homosexual Practice: Texts and Hermeneutics* (Nashville, TN: Abingdon Press, 2002), 303–336.

word is used in other places in the Bible. It is only used twice in the New Testament, both referring to the soft clothing that pampered, rich people wear in kings' palaces in contrast to John the Baptizer's bold and courageous prophetic identity. A certain kind of fastidiousness about clothing and appearance is effeminate in men, not to be confused with the fully masculine wisdom found in many of the manual arts (e.g., Exod. 31:3, 35:31). The Old Testament uses a related word, *rok*, a number of times which is translated as "weakness, sickness, or disease," and the root simply means "soft, tender, or fainthearted." That word can also refer to benign forms of youth or gentleness (which is a fruit of the Spirit), but in a number of places indicates a sinful softness and cowardice. When an army was mustered for war, Moses instructs the officers to speak to the people and say, "Is there any man who is fearful and *fainthearted*? Let him go back to his house, lest he make the heart of his fellows melt like his own" (Deut. 20:8, ESV, emphasis mine). Or as we noted above, men who run away from battle in fear are likened to women (Is. 19:16, Jer. 50:37, 51:30).

To our point here, it's rather striking that in John's vision of the New Jerusalem coming down out of Heaven as a bride adorned for her Husband, John looks away for a moment and sees those who are left outside of that glory. He writes, "But as for the cowardly, the faithless, the detestable, as for murderers, the sexually immoral, sorcerers, idolaters, and all liars, their portion will be in the lake that burns with fire and sulfur, which is the second death" (Rev. 21:8, ESV). Notice the very front of the line, at the top of the list of those outside the city: the *cowardly*. The cowardly are not *inside* the city, honoring the Bride. Men are called to a masculine-shaped courage that faces challenges, problems, difficulties, enemies, and threats with joy and courage. And it is that courage that will live forever inside the New Jerusalem. Whether the threat is external or internal, financial or familial, political or emotional or medical, a man does his duty and uses whatever strength God has given him to protect those around him. A man does not run from the fight. A man does not shrink back, whether in the woods or the shop or the gym or on the couch. Sometimes a man is tempted to do masculine-looking things only as a distraction tactic. *I don't have time for my wife's concerns, I need to go hunting. I can't discipline my kids, I need to read this fat theology book.* That is effeminate, too. Masculine strength understands which responsibilities are most pressing and prioritizes biblically. On the other hand, a man who never cultivates the masculine virtues of self-sufficiency, self-discipline, and self-defense is on a path of Charmin softness and really should change course.

All of this is why, the harebrained imaginations of Hollywood to the contrary, a literal army of women does not stand a chance against an army of men. This is why there are no all-women football teams in the NFL. Well, at least there aren't any yet at the time of this writing, but if there ever are, I am reasonably confident those women will be hopped up on unnatural doses of *male* hormones. This is why the introduction of women into the American military and police forces is not only a shame and an abomination, it is also a certain *weakening* and *softening* of our national and local defenses. Now that I've secured this book for some future hate-banning, I might as well come out and say what I really think, which is that just because something is weaker doesn't mean it is of less value. The really bizarre thing is people who want to make males the ideal human being, as if being "as strong as" men makes you more of a person. But that's just silly—and actually sexist, as they say. The reverse would be like men feeling insecure because they can't ovulate as well as women.

But the command here is that men, and husbands in particular, are required by God to *honor* the weakness of their wife, which, on the surface of it, seems strange to men. Most women would never think twice about the fact that they are weaker than men (being the reasonable and rational creatures that they are), but men are the kind of people who often find weakness offensive, and, ironically, I highly suspect it's a bunch of male pastors and male seminary professors and male politicians who have taught women to be deeply offended by Peter's statement here.

So why should we honor weakness? Isn't weakness bad, unhelpful, and a liability? Well, we can speak of at least two kinds of weakness. One kind is sinful and needs overcoming and truly is an unhelpful vulnerability. When Jesus was praying in the garden, He urged His disciples to stay awake and pray with Him, "Watch and pray, lest you enter into temptation. The spirit indeed is willing, but the flesh is weak" (Matt. 26:41, NKJV). There are various weaknesses that are a result of sin and are themselves sinful. To fail to resist temptation to envy or worry or lust is to sin. That kind of weakness must be repented of. All Christians must exercise themselves to grow strong in holiness in order to resist that kind of weakness and temptation.

The second kind of weakness spoken of in the Bible is a creational weakness. Paul talks this way in 1 Corinthians 12: "And the eye cannot say unto the hand, I have no need of thee: nor again the head to the feet, I have no need of you. Nay, much more those members of the body, which seem to be more feeble, are necessary" (vv. 21–22). An eye is not as physically strong as a hand, but a hand is not nearly as good at seeing as an eye. These are creational differences and relative weaknesses, and Paul is talking about different people in the body of Christ, different people in the Church, all of whom are necessary.

Husbands are exhorted by Peter not to despise the fact that their wives are weaker than they are, but to honor them. They have less testosterone so that they can nurture life inside themselves. They are weaker in certain ways so that they can actually be stronger in other ways. "By faith Sarah herself also received *strength* to conceive seed, and she bore a child when she was past the age, because she judged Him faithful who had promised" (Heb. 11:11, NKJV emphasis mine).

Men, this means that you must not resent the fact that your wife (or wife-to-be) is a woman. You must not resent the fact that she needs your help. Honor the fact that she needs your help. That's why God made you strong. That's what your strength is for. Delight to help her. This doesn't mean that she needs to pretend to be a child or that you need to micromanage her life as though she were a child. Part of helping her and washing her with the water of the Word should mean that over time she is growing in wisdom and certain skills and abilities in running her home well. But the old customs of opening doors, carrying groceries, and walking nearest to traffic on the sidewalk were ways our culture marked this honor due to women. The way a man ultimately honors the glorious weakness of a woman is by laying his life down for hers. When a man stands between his woman and danger, when a man gives up a spot on a lifeboat for a woman, he is saying that his life is more disposable than hers. And it is. This is what the strength of men is *for*. The strength of men is for dying, for sacrifice, for provision, and for protection. While a man may be stronger, his life is less necessary for the continuation of the human race. This is the point of honoring your wife as the weaker vessel.

While I'm here, if I may be allowed to run back around the other side of this point, I would also encourage wives (and those preparing to be wives) not to resent the fact that you are marrying a *man*. I touched on this earlier, but it's worth noting again: God calls you to respect your man *as a man*. This means, among other things, that God has wired him to focus on particular tasks, generally speaking, *one at a time*. This, if you can get your head around it, is actually one of the strengths of men. We tend to focus on one problem, one mission, and simply don't think about anything else. This is what allows men to run into battle, focused on their duty and mission. It was a bunch of men who probably didn't bathe or shave or think about much else for a long time who put other men on the moon. There was also an army of women thinking of all the other things keeping them alive.

When your husband says that he was working on something at work and forgot to call, that's probably true. He likely didn't nefariously *plan* not to call you. Or if you ask him what he was thinking about and he says "Nothing"—it probably was nothing. Do not imagine that he thinks like a woman or feels like a woman or intuits like a woman. When something isn't right, it may be perfectly obvious to you (or to any other woman), but it may not be perfectly obvious to him (or any other man). Do not despise his masculinity. Do not mock it. How could he not know how you're feeling about the mashed potatoes or your dress or the kids? Well, *part* of the answer is mysteriously embedded in his XY chromosomes. He was probably thinking about how to fix your car or how to pay for something your family needs. Please don't misunderstand me: a man certainly does have a responsibility to communicate with his wife, he needs to remember to call if that was the agreement, to ask a lot of questions, and to grow in his ability to sense the situation. But a wife also has a responsibility to respect her man's masculinity and his calling to be a man.

All of this is to say that a fair bit of marital conflict arises from a subtle resentment of the fact that your spouse is a different sex than you. Which, if you think about it, is really funny. Do you want your husband to be a woman? Do you want your wife to be a man? Yeah, I didn't think so. So learn to laugh with God about how He made the world and created people, male and female, and invented this crazy thing called marriage. What a hilarious joke. What glorious fun.

We need to note one more thing about this difference. We honor the difference, this relative weakness, because this inequality is the basis for all civilizational *fruitfulness*. This is literally the case in marriage, through the gift of children, but this is also the source of so much human creativity, productivity, and wealth. Different people with different strengths and weaknesses see the world differently, think differently, and have different skills and abilities. This is the basis for inventions, improvements, and all sorts of discoveries. Men, when you honor the weakness of your wife, you are honoring the principle of productivity, fruitfulness, and industry. Your wife is the kind of person who makes people inside of her. There is nothing in all of creation as valuable or marvelous as a human being, no mere mortal, made in the image of the infinite God. It doesn't seem to be an accident at all that the New Jerusalem is both a city and a bride coming down out of Heaven (Rev. 21:2). When a husband resolutely and consistently honors his wife, he is building Christian civilization. If the city of God is built by Christ using His strength to sacrificially love His bride, the Christian Church, then every man who imitates that strong love to honor his bride is participating in that great building project.

Next, Peter explains that the "honor" due to the wife is to be measured by the law of love: "love your neighbor as yourself," or, as Peter puts it, "as being heirs together of the grace of life." The logic of the verse is that a husband is required by God to honor his wife as the weaker vessel, precisely because she is an heir of the grace of life together with him. Whatever her relative weakness, God values her the same as you. The same precious blood was shed for her sins as for your own. And if God valued her, you must value her. If she is valuable in His sight, she must be valuable in your sight. So speak to her and about her as a co-heir of the grace of life. Honor her as one who has inherited eternal life, as an eternal soul who will live forever. She is no mere mortal. God lives inside of her, and one day she will be raised into an everlasting state of glory that will cause you to tremble.

This runs directly into the final warning, "that your prayers be not hindered." It's quite possible that Peter simply means that men who are disobedient in how they treat their wives will be the kind of men who don't pray, or at least don't pray well. It's possible that Peter merely means a sort of correlation: men who don't honor their wives don't tend to honor God. But I suspect that the connection is more causative than merely correlative. And there's good textual reasons for suspecting that.

Running through the New Testament are a number of texts that explicitly promise that God will treat us the way we treat others. "But if you do not forgive, neither will your Father in heaven forgive your trespasses" (Mk. 11:26, NKJV). Likewise, in the parable of the sheep and the goats, Jesus expressly says, "Assuredly, I say to you, inasmuch as you did it to one of the least of these My brethren, you did it to Me." (Matt. 25:40, NKJV). Jesus says that He receives what we do to others as having been done to Him, and as we treat others, we are inviting God to treat us the same. When Jesus confronted Paul on the road to Damascus, He asked him, "Saul, Saul, why are you persecuting Me?" (Acts 9:4, ESV) Jesus took personally Saul's persecution of Christians. John expresses a similar sentiment: "He who does not love his brother whom he has seen, how can he love God whom he has not seen?" (1 Jn. 4:20, NKJV) How can you say you love God whom you have not seen, if you do not love your wife whom you have seen?

All of this is to say that this warning means that God will not listen to the prayers of men who dishonor their wives. Or, we might say that you are asking God to listen to you about as well as you listen to your wife. How much care and attention do you want God to give to you and your prayers? Then give that kind of care and attention to your wife and her concerns and requests.

QUESTIONS FOR DISCUSSION

1. What does it mean that women are the "weaker vessel"? What does it mean that the glory of men is their strength? Do you agree?

2. What are different kinds of weakness and which one are husbands required to honor in their wives? What are some ways men honor that weakness today or in the past?

3. How should wives honor the masculinity of their husbands?

4. How is honoring weakness/difference actually honoring the principle of fruitfulness and productivity?

5. What does the warning, "that your prayers be not hindered," mean?

CHAPTER 15

BIRTH CONTROL, BABIES, AND BARRENNESS

O NE of the things you have hopefully discussed already is the matter of birth control and babies. And while this is not the stuff of first dates, it really should be something you've discussed by the time you're engaged. But we live in days of mass confusion even inside the Christian Church, and so we really shouldn't assume anything.

First off, since we are Christians, we should be committed to believing whatever the Bible says and obeying it. Wherever the Bible is silent, we should conclude that this is because God has left the matter to the discretion, wisdom, and sound reasoning of His people. In other words, we are bound by God's Word, but wherever God has not spoken, His people are free. So, what has God said about babies and birth control? He has said a lot about babies, and He has said next to nothing about birth control. At the same time, it should not be irrelevant to us who is championing birth control. If the worshippers of Molech are the purveyors of birth control, we really should be skeptical, since they are also the ones passing their sons through the fire to their idols. Margaret Sanger, the founder of Planned Parenthood, was one of the earliest champions of birth control *and abortion*. Let the reader understand.

However, we really do need to walk through this whole matter carefully.

The Bible opens with a command that clearly implies children: "And God blessed them, and God said unto them, Be fruitful, and multiply, and replenish the earth, and subdue it: and have dominion over the fish of the sea, and over the fowl of the air, and over every living thing that moveth upon the earth" (Gen. 1:28). So we gather from this verse that having babies is one of the jobs of the human race and of married couples specifically. This job is itself a great *blessing*, and those who take it up in faith are blessed. This job goes together with taking dominion over the whole earth and ruling it well. People are essential for the job of caring for the earth and causing it to be fruitful. It was (and is) a big world with lots of things to discover, invent, study, organize, beautify, and tame, and that takes lots of man-hours, which requires lots of people, which, to put the matter frankly, requires lots of sex. And that was God's idea.

We also know that Adam sinned, and this resulted in a cursed world. God promised that He would undo the curse of the serpent through the seed of the woman, which is to say that salvation would come through *childbearing* (Gen. 3:15). The curse of sin included death, difficulty in working the earth, and the fact that women would experience a lot more pain in childbearing: "I will greatly multiply thy sorrow and thy conception; in sorrow thou shalt bring forth children ..." (Gen. 3:16). We see here in the first three chapters of the Bible the basic shape of the whole biblical testimony on this topic. Children are a great blessing from the Lord, and they are a particular blessing for working the earth given all the weeds and thorns as well as a central part of God's plan of redemption, but the pain and difficulty of childbearing must also be taken into account by wise and godly men.

Therefore, we should celebrate and believe what the psalmist sings: "Behold, children are a heritage from the LORD, the fruit of the womb is a reward. Like arrows in the hand of a warrior, so are the children of one's youth. Happy is the man who has his quiver full of them; they shall not be ashamed, but shall speak with their enemies in the gate" (Ps. 127:3–5, NKJV). Christians must not be ashamed of loving children, welcoming children, and driving large vans full of them. Christians must rejoice in the awkward stares of people at the shopping mall and the snide comments about where they come from. The Bible says that children are a *reward*, arrows in the hand of a warrior, and they will stand with us against our enemies. If the modern Church is impotent in our

stand against cultural apostasy, should we really be surprised when the modern Church has largely succumbed
to a worldly sexual impotence? We must value what God
values, love what God loves, and believe what God says
is true in order to wield real biblical power and authority.
And the Bible clearly teaches that children are central to
biblical power and authority.

Nevertheless, the Bible also clearly commands men
to provide for their families. Paul says that this is central to being a *Christian*: "But if any provide not for his
own, and specially for those of his own house, he hath
denied the faith, and is worse than an infidel" (1 Tim.
5:8). Men who father children without thought or serious
care for their provision are wicked fools. Paul says that
failure to provide for them is worse than being a run-
of-the-mill pagan. What does this provision include? We
have noted previously that the command for husbands to
love their wives as their own bodies included nourishing
and cherishing (Eph. 5:29), which literally means feeding and keeping warm. This must also be understood to
include a thoroughly Christian education for all his children: "And you, fathers, do not provoke your children,
but bring them up in the training and admonition of the
Lord" (Eph. 6:4, NKJV). It does not seem to be an accident
that the same word for "nurture" that Paul said husbands
were responsible to provide for their wives is used here
for "training" children. A man must provide a thorough
Christian education for his children, and he must not
send them to Molech's government schools to be trained
in secular humanism (and more on that in Chapter 17).

This provision that a man is responsible to provide also includes wise and biblical medical attention and health care. A man must protect his wife just as he would protect his own life (Eph. 5:28). While we live in anti-child times, and many medical professionals are hyper risk-averse, the historic rates of maternal mortality are not irrelevant. If a medical professional, especially a Bible-believing OB/GYN, recommends against a woman having any more children, I do not see how a man who decides to have a medical procedure done to prevent future pregnancies for the health and safety and provision of his wife and family can be accused of being anti-life or anti-children. He is taking the curse of sin seriously and taking steps to mitigate it. But this is not the same thing as refusing to welcome children because your wife might gain some weight and that might lead to hypertension and that might lead to a greater risk of heart disease. Living is dangerous and making new immortal people is difficult work. And Christians should be known for their courage. Bearing children faithfully really does require courage. Of course there is a difference between facing reasonable risks and complete folly. Nevertheless, if it is not medically wise to continue bearing biological children, there are other avenues of fruitful childrearing ministry in Christian schools, homeschool co-ops, Sunday school, foster care, and adoption.

Therefore, Christians should take all of this together and be the kind of people who love children, and getting married should ordinarily mean planning to start a family and welcoming children. The modern notion of getting married and then thinking about having a family at some point down the road is utterly foreign to Scripture. While I wouldn't bind anyone's conscience over whether it is wise to wait a year before having kids in order to get to know one another first, if you don't think you know one another well enough already, why are you getting married now? And furthermore, what makes you think being alone without children will actually accomplish your goal of getting to know one another better? In the biblical way of thinking, other people actually contribute to making us who we are. By God's design that often happens best with small people who look a lot like us. In the Bible, barrenness is part of the curse, and not something to embrace, even temporarily.

This is a book written by a pastor, not a doctor or medical professional, and so I strongly recommend that you also seek out godly and biblically informed medical advice. But I can say that if you are considering using some form of birth control that you be aware of the fact that not all birth control is created equal. There is good reason to be highly skeptical of most chemical and hormonal forms of birth control. Take the fact that we hardly understand how hormones work, add to this a fair bit of modern medical hubris, then pour on all of our current abortion and trans-mutilation madness, and that's a cocktail worth immediately tossing into the garbage. Barrier methods of birth control are fairly simple and straightforward (if cumbersome). But at least you can see what you're doing to your body, and the effects are right there in front of you. "Natural family planning" is another way conscientious Christian couples sometimes exercise dominion in this area. Natural family planning relies on couples tracking where a woman is in her cycle and avoiding sexual relations during her days of fertility. It's my own personal and pastoral opinion that we don't really know what we're doing to female bodies with hormonal birth control, and a woman's chemical and hormonal balance is already a wonderfully complex and mysterious balance. Why would we think it's a good idea to suppress or reverse it? Some women, having been on the Pill for years, are startled and troubled to find it difficult to conceive after coming off the Pill. We live in a political and cultural environment highly incentivized not to tell us the truth about possible side-effects and long-term consequences of the Pill. If hormonal birth control was connected to higher incidence of, say, breast cancer, you can bet that such a study would be the thing being heavily suppressed. Not only that, but some hormonal forms of birth control are expressly abortifacients, meaning that if there is "breakthrough ovulation," and conception occurs, the "birth control" will abort the newly conceived child. These forms of birth control are clearly immoral and not options for Bible-believing Christians.

The morning-after pill is also not birth control; it is an abortion drug. However, Christians should also be aware that other forms of hormonal birth control, including the Pill, list thinning the uterine lining to prevent implantation as an intended effect. If that is true, no thoughtful Christian should want to knowingly put something in their body that could make the intended home for a child uninhabitable.

IUDs are also known to advertise this as one of its effects; these devices that are implanted inside a woman's uterus also seem to have a higher incidence of other complications. All this to say, do your homework, get biblical counsel, think like a Christian, and then act in faith. You cannot possibly know everything there is to know, and no doubt, generations from now will understand all of this better than we do, but we can seek to be faithful with the information the Lord has provided in obedience to His clear Word.

Bear with me for a moment on this tangent: One of the words that marks a biblical wisdom is the word "better." Wisdom refuses to sacrifice the good on the altar of "the best." While Christians should be people who strive for excellence, even perfection, perfection*ism* is one of the greatest enemies of real gospel progress. "Good" is still better than many other options. In other words, many situations need to be evaluated with the question, "Compared to what?" A whole lot of sorrow and regret might be avoided by recognizing that many situations are better than what they might be, while not giving an inch to apathy or laziness. Proverbs is full of "better than" statements. Wisdom is better than silver or gold (Prov. 3:13–14). It's better to be disliked and able to pay your bills than to think highly of yourself and be poor (Prov. 12:9). Better to have corn dogs on paper plates with love than steak on fine china where there is hatred (Prov. 15:17). And similarly, it's better to have a bowl of cereal in peace than an overflowing pantry with constant strife (Prov. 17:1). Proverbs also says that where there are no oxen, the trough is clean; but much increase comes by the strength of an ox (Prov. 14:4). My point is that we want to think in biblical categories about having children. Better is a passel of kids than a boat and a motorcycle. Better is the strength of children than a living room that could be on HGTV. Better is a happy home full of laughing mouths eating oatmeal for breakfast than the silence of bitterness poured over gourmet delicacies with a beach-babe body.

However, in all of these "better than" scenarios there are more than two options actually possible. There are actually always a total of four options when there are two variables. Options could include 1) no children and hatred, 2) lots of children and hatred, 3) no children and love, and 4) lots of children and love. We can easily eliminate the worst option: no children and lots of hatred. That's bad. And don't choose a big house, a third car, or a vacation home in the Bahamas over children. People are immortals. People will live forever. Houses, cars, and vacation homes will not. Do the math, silly. We should also recognize that God is the Lord of the womb (more about this shortly). He opens the womb and closes it, and sometimes He does not give biological children. In those cases, it is absolutely better to be childless and walking in the love of the Lord than to be childless and bitter. But I also want to point out in all of this that a pile of kids is not an *automatic* blessing. The blessings of God are not mechanical. They do not drop out of Heaven like a can of Coke out of a soda machine. The blessings of God must be received by faith and with thanksgiving and in the fear of God. As Pastor Douglas Wilson has pointed out, the High Priest Eli would not have been *more* faithful had he fathered *more* unfaithful sons.

So the best scenario is a van full of kids *and* overflowing gospel joy. But in a fallen world where pain in childbirth has been multiplied, and where God has not expressly forbidden people from doing anything to space children out or take medical action to be done having kids, a godly man should monitor the spiritual and physical health of his wife and kids as he builds his household. Taking dominion does not mean barking orders or breeding thoughtlessly. It means dwelling with your wife according to knowledge (1 Pet. 3:7). It means knowing your field, knowing your wife, knowing your kids, and trying to maximize your fruitfulness in this world, for their good, for the glory of God, and for the expansion of His Kingdom. Do not be like the man who does not count the cost, cannot finish what he has started, becomes a mockery of a Christian family, and puts the name of Christ to shame (Lk. 14:28–30). But do not be the timid, unfaithful servant who buried his talent in the ground either (Matt. 25:14–30).

With that said, I must conclude this chapter with a section on bearing with barrenness. Part of the curse of sin is the presence of barrenness in the world. Sometimes there are clear medical causes, and sometimes barrenness is a mystery. The Bible actually says a fair bit about this reality, enough to make barrenness a scriptural theme. So we should familiarize ourselves with it when discussing Christian marriage.

While modern medical science gives us a great deal to be thankful for in understanding fertility, conception, pregnancy, etc., the Bible still clearly teaches that it is God who opens and closes the womb (Ruth 4:13). So "planning" to have children should be held loosely, as with all our plans, and we should make it our habit to say, "if the Lord wills" (Jas. 4:13–15). We have all heard some couple announce confidently that they are planning to have their first child next April, and in the providence of God, sometimes they are right! But we have also probably all known someone who announced something like that, maybe even the opposite, that they are planning to "wait" for a year or two to have children, and then— ta-da!—they are pregnant the next month. This doesn't mean that pregnancy is inscrutable and mysterious. We do know how babies happen—mostly! But the point is simply that God is Lord over it all. He opens and closes the womb (Gen. 29:31, 30:22), and so we should seek to be faithful and fruitful while holding the whole thing up to the Lord with open hands, not imagining that we have somehow gotten control of this baby business.

"So Boaz took Ruth, and she was his wife: and when he went in unto her, the LORD gave her conception, and she bare a son" (Ruth 4:13). Recall too that Ruth was a widow and, apparently, she had previously been barren. This theme of barrenness runs throughout the Bible and is directly related to God's promise to Eve that she would bear a seed that would crush the head of the dragon. But this promise was made in the midst of the curses for sin on the ground and the womb. God promised fruitfulness in the midst of the barrenness of sin. This underlines the fact that salvation would be all of grace. Salvation would only come by God's supernatural intervention in human history. God would have to make our barren land and barren wombs fruitful. This theme creates one of the central tension points in the Old Testament story. Sarah was barren, but God had promised Abraham descendants as numerous as the stars of Heaven and that all the nations would be blessed in his seed. This is the tension of living in this world, barren in sin, and yet a recipient of God's gracious promises to bless us anyway. When Sarah conceives Isaac, his name meaning "laughter" reflects not merely the joy of bearing a child but also the joy of God's covenant promises being fulfilled. Likewise, Hannah was barren (like Israel) and when she conceived Samuel, it was a sign that God was hearing the cries of all His people to save them from their enemies (1 Sam. 2).

Barrenness represents the cursed ground. It does not merely represent the cursed ground, it is *part* of the cursed ground. What was made to be fruitful is fruitless. It is a double curse to *choose* barrenness, to *choose* to be childless. It is a far greater tragedy when that barrenness is chosen by intentionally taking the life of a child already conceived (abortion), but it is still a tragedy when a couple castrate themselves intentionally.

For most women, the natural pain of barrenness is a deep grief. "There are three things that are never satisfied, yea, four things say not, it is enough: the grave; and the barren womb; the earth that is not filled with water; and the fire that saith not, it is enough" (Prov. 30:15–16).

Sometimes barrenness is for a season and sometimes it is lifelong. But the gospel is here in a very tangible way. It was for the barrenness of this world, the barrenness of human hearts, that Jesus came. If we are reading our Bibles carefully, we ought to see the pattern of God giving barren wives conception as a sign that He is answering prayer to deliver and save His people (e.g., Judg. 13:2–3).

In fact, Luke highlights this fact in the barrenness of Elisabeth and Zachariah (Lk. 1:7). The fact that Elisabeth conceived in her old age was a sign that God was once again acting decisively to save His people. The angel specifically points to Elisabeth's barrenness and subsequent conception as part of the evidence for Mary's *virgin* conception. In this way, we ought to see the virgin conception of Jesus as the conception that all the other barren conceptions were pointing toward. The barrenness of this world was *worse* than all the barren wombs. In all of those conceptions, a man descended from Adam still fathered the child, passing his sin and guilt down through natural generation. But in the virgin conception, God acted even more supernaturally, fathering a child by the power of the Holy Spirit, begetting a truly human son without a human father. So it is that every true Christian has been begotten again by the same sort of miracle: "But as many as received Him, to them He gave the right to become children of God, to those who believe in His name: who were born, not of blood, nor of the will of the flesh, nor of the will of man, but of God" (Jn. 1:12–13, NKJV). Every true Christian has been born again, not by natural generation—we are barren

and impotent to save ourselves—but only by the supernatural intervention of God.

Lastly, I'll return to a point made briefly earlier in
this chapter: In every hardship, remember the wisdom
of "better than" applies. God's plan is "better than" our
plans. Whatever God gives us is for our good. Whether
He gives a passel of kids, only one, or none of our own
biological children, His plan is better than our plan. This
was the lesson that Naomi learned through her trials and
God's blessing on Ruth: God was better to her than sev-
en sons (Ruth 4:15). Isaiah promises that, in the Messiah, God will make even the eunuchs fruitful, blessing
them with homes and names better than that of sons and
daughters (Is. 56:5). "For it is written: 'Rejoice, O barren,
You who do not bear! Break forth and shout, you who
are not in labor! For the desolate has many more children Than she who has a husband.' Now we, brethren, as
Isaac was, are children of promise" (Gal. 4:27–28, quoting Is. 56:6). Whether through teaching Sunday school,
foster care, adoption, or biological conception and birth,
to those who trust in His name, "He grants the barren
woman a home, like a joyful mother of children. Praise
the LORD!" (Ps. 113:9, NKJV).

QUESTIONS FOR DISCUSSION

1. *What should the general attitude of Christians be toward children and birth control, and why?*

2. *What do the first three chapters of Genesis teach us generally about children and childbearing? How do those chapters help us frame the discussion of children and birth control?*

3. *Why might Christians have a particular skepticism about chemical/hormonal forms of birth control?*

4. *Explain the "better than" principle from Proverbs and how it applies to thinking about children.*

5. *What does the Bible teach about barrenness? How does it point to the gospel?*

CHAPTER 16

HOW FAR IS TOO FAR?

MODERN American culture is a sexual cesspool. From movies, to sitcoms, to pornography, to magazines, to social media and the internet, to casual hookup and shack-up culture, to the so-called alphabet soup of sexual perversions, you can barely make it through a day without smelling the stench of our cultural hatred of the marriage bed. These days, it seems like some kind of miracle if a story is told in a movie or novel of a man and a woman remaining chaste until they are married.

Given the cesspool, it can be a real challenge not only to remain pure before marriage, but also to even know what purity means before and leading up to your wedding night. *Can we kiss? Can we make out? Can we experiment sexually just a little, as long as we don't go "all the way"?*

This chapter will necessarily be a bit PG-13, but not pornographic and not needlessly lurid, but hopefully it will be direct and plain in a helpful way. Some of what follows I will connect to explicit biblical teaching, but some of what follows will be my pastoral advice, which is merely that: advice. While this chapter begins addressing those who are striving for purity while preparing for marriage, it concludes with a general word of hope and exhortation for all sexual sinners, married or not.

First off, we live in a world where we really need to explain and understand the sin of fornication. The Greek word *porneas* can have a broad and general meaning of any form of sexual immorality, but it can also have a narrower meaning, from which we derive the English word "fornication," which is, properly speaking, any sexual activity prior to or outside the bounds of marriage. Paul lists fornication as one of the works of the flesh: "Now the works of the flesh are evident, which are: adultery, fornication, uncleanness, lewdness" (Gal. 5:19, NKJV). Likewise, Paul says Christians shouldn't even talk in a way that arouses or makes light of sexual sins: "But fornication and all uncleanness or covetousness, let it not even be named among you, as is fitting for saints; neither filthiness, nor foolish talking, nor coarse jesting, which are not fitting, but rather giving of thanks" (Eph. 5:3–4, NKJV). Fornication is one of the sins a Christian is to put to death: "Therefore put to death your members which are on the earth: fornication, uncleanness, passion, evil desire, and covetousness, which is idolatry" (Col. 3:5, NKJV). Finally, "Marriage is honorable among all, and the bed undefiled; but fornicators and adulterers God will judge" (Heb. 13:4, NKJV). This last passage is a key one: marriage is to be honored by all, and there are two principle ways it can be dishonored: fornication and adultery. Fornication is any and all sexual sin outside of a marriage covenant. Adultery is sinning against an existing marriage covenant.

So then, when has fornication occurred? Is kissing fornication? What about holding hands? What about texting sexual messages to one another or sending sexual pictures? Without going beyond clear Scripture, we can draw a pretty direct analogy from what Jesus says about lust and adultery: if you look at a woman to lust after her, you have already committed adultery with her in your heart (Matt. 5:28). The principle is that you may not lust after that which has not been given to you. If you are already married to someone else or if she is, then it is not lawful to lust after her because she belongs to another man, you belong to another woman, and that is adulterous lust (Matt. 5:27–28).

It is a slightly different situation when you have asked a woman to marry you and she has said yes, and her parents have given their blessing, and you've reserved the church for the ceremony. But the fact remains that she has not yet been *given* to you. Her breasts do not yet belong to you. And so lust is still a sin. The sin of lust is not the mere presence of desire. Everyone knows that a man who asks a woman to marry him desires to sleep with that woman. And the woman who agrees to marry a man is agreeing to sleep with that man, and she desires to do so as well. It is not the mere presence of desire, even sexual desire, that is sinful, but it is the *indulgence* of sexual desire or pleasure for someone who has not (yet) been given to you for that purpose. This means we must flee all sexual arousal for anyone other than our spouse, which would include heavy make-out sessions, taking off clothes, putting hands inside of clothes, and every sort of creative petting or oral sex. But remember that Jesus says that this lust can be as hidden as a lurking thought in the heart of man. Therefore, Jesus says to cut off the hand that causes you to sin and pluck out the eye that causes you to sin. Do whatever it takes to avoid situations where any sexual sin is likely or possible. Make like Joseph and run away from Potiphar's wife. For this reason, sexual texting is completely out and probably most sexy pictures, unless your mother would approve and is in the group text (kidding! but not really). By the way, this isn't the point of this chapter or this book, but if all of this is Christian living for engaged couples, it goes double for single folks (or couples not yet engaged).

I would also argue that you ought not start anything that would be unlawful for you to finish. There is a huge difference between kissing your fiancée goodnight on the doorstep on the one hand, and fogging up the windshield while parked somewhere in seclusion, on the other. Without creating a list of extra-biblical rules, my general recommendation is that couples not act in ways that simulate married life, thus inviting such situations. For example, just because you are engaged doesn't mean it's okay or reasonable to go on vacation together, so long as you are in separate beds. My pastoral advice would be to not even spend long periods of time alone in private places together, e.g., alone in your apartment or her apartment. Remember that we are complex beings, body, soul, and spirit, and you should not underestimate how external circumstances invite trajectories. Same thing goes for the emotional and spiritual sides of things. Some Christians are already emotionally sleeping together long before marriage, and they wonder why they are struggling so much sexually. Yes, it is important to be growing together emotionally, but if you are undressing your souls to one another, you are practicing something that will likely make it harder to keep your actual clothes on.

Even spiritually, it's important to remember that a man is not a woman's spiritual head until after the vows have been exchanged. There is a sense in which a couple is beginning to practice life together, but even here, it can be a tricky balancing act. It would be strange not to be growing more comfortable and intimate as the wedding day approaches, but couples really do need to exercise wisdom in the timing of things. Someone once said you should think of it like unrolling a carpet: you want to unroll both ends at roughly the same rate so as to not get all catawampus. Think of the emotional, spiritual, and physical elements of the relationship developing at roughly the same rate. If one side is accelerated, it naturally begs the other side to follow along at the same rate. If your wedding is tomorrow, that's one thing, but if it's in another three months, you might be in trouble. Because of the union of the various elements that make us human, even spiritual communion between a man and a woman is not unrelated to sexual union.

My point is not that every form of spiritual fellowship is heading to bed. Of course not. My point is merely that people need to be careful, thoughtful, wise, and not dumb. But many Christians are perilously naïve, thinking that if they are praying together or reading their Bibles together they will automatically be less likely to sleep together before they are married. Of course, keeping Christ central is an important part of fighting temptation and preparing for marriage, but so is a bit of common sense. And the fact of the matter is, without common sense, all that praying and Bible reading can just as easily be another form of foreplay.

A few other points here.

First, it really is worth fighting for purity *now*, before your wedding night. You are practicing now for purity inside your marriage. You cannot dishonor and defile the marriage bed now and then expect for it to be magically holy on your wedding night. In other words, just because you're going to be lawfully wedded in six weeks doesn't make your fornication last night less sinful or less problematic. Giving in to lust now is actually practicing to give in to lust later. But sin doesn't care about boundaries or distinctions. Sin may tempt you by saying that it doesn't matter that much since you'll be married soon, but sin doesn't actually care about marriage vows. The same sin will pop up inside marriage, after you are married, tempting you to look at other women, other men, movies, pictures, etc. So what are you practicing now?

Are you practicing self-control? Are you practicing to keep your vows, to honor the marriage bed and keep it undefiled? Or are you practicing for adultery?

Second, and related to all of this, is my strongest plea to have a zero tolerance policy for pornography. In this world, pornography is everywhere. We live in a pornographic culture. And while the temptation can afflict some women, this is a great affliction for men in particular because God has generally wired men in a far more visual way and because the sex drive of men tends to be far more intense and simplistic. It is a very rare man in our day who has not struggled with temptation to look at porn at some point in his life. But the same point I made above applies here: Porn is terrible preparation for marriage. Looking at porn and masturbating is a form a fornication. Hopefully, God has granted you a measure of purity and victory over lust and pornography if you are now engaged and preparing for marriage. But let me make this point clearly: if you have been given over to the sin of pornography, falling into it regularly, you are not in a good position to get married. In fact, if up to this point, this subject hasn't been brought up, but you know it's an ongoing problem for you, I would urge you to reach out for a pastoral opinion on your situation. It may be better to postpone your wedding to get this sin dealt with before starting life together in the quicksand of a longstanding porn habit.

On the one hand, the fact that a man fights such temptations tells you that he is a man—that he is male—and that he needs to get married. The Bible clearly says that it is not good for man to be alone, and his strong sex drive is surely part of why it is not good for him to be alone. Paul also says that it is better to marry than to burn with lust, specifically for those struggling with sexual self-control (1 Cor. 7:9). Therefore, marriage is one lawful solution to the temptation to lust. On the other hand, marriage should not be thought of as the solve-all for habitual lust. The man who has habitually given in to lust will not magically discover self-control simply because he wore a tux in a church and made some vows. The same lack of self-control that led to habitual porn use will kick in shortly and make keeping those vows next to impossible. And women really need to understand that they certainly can be part of a biblical solution to temptation, but they ought not think they can be the entire solution. What godly men and women and their parents and pastors should want to have some measure of certainty about is not perfection or sinlessness, but rather a clear and growing evidence over some time of the work of the Spirit giving the fruit of self-control, the ability to say no to sin, and a distinct hatred for that particular form of sin.

Sexual lust is a species of covetousness, which Paul says is idolatry (Col. 3:5). At the center of sexual lust is an idol of pleasure, happiness, and fulfillment that is a black hole of despair and death (Prov. 5:5, 7:27). Like most drugs, sexual highs demand a constant increase. What was stimulating one week won't be good enough the next. Idols are man-made images that pretend to be real, that pretend to communicate life, but they cannot. They have eyes and hands and mouths, but they cannot see, cannot touch, cannot taste (Ps. 115:4–7). And all those who make them and serve them become like them (Ps. 115:8). Idols slowly but surely destroy our humanity. Men given over to pornography are slowly being unmanned, dehumanized, and emasculated.

Pornography is also a false catechism. It is not teaching you how to love a real woman or a real man; it is not teaching you what real, godly sex is actually like. It's a *graven* image, and therefore it is a false picture of sexuality. Like all idolatry, it is ultimately a form of self-worship. Who picks the picture? Who chooses the video clip? Who decides what is good and what is pleasing? It is the viewer *himself*. The viewer, the *voyeur*, is the god of that sexual experience, dictating when and where and how. But marital love that is blessed by God is between two distinct persons with particular personalities, desires, interests, preferences, and challenges! *Real* people are not so simple, not so "on-demand." Real love means learning how another person is different from you, learning to meet their needs, learning to see what is best for them. Real love requires patience, kindness, gentleness, and self-sacrifice.

Pornography is not only terrible preparation for a real, biblical sexual relationship, it is a predominantly *masculine* perversion of sexual love. Pornography is a thoroughly perverted masculine fantasy, presenting women as men sinfully want them, not as women truly desire to be cherished, protected, courted, and loved. Therefore, porn is misogynistic; but also, and quite ironically, latently homosexual, despite the complicity of all the willing women in the industry. Porn is driven by the lusts and imaginations of *men*: men are often the ones taking the pictures, producing the movies, making the websites, and men are the ones picking and choosing and serving themselves as they indulge their lusts. Even when the pornography is technically heterosexual, there's something deeply homosexual about the whole enterprise: men serving up sexual pleasure for other men.

In addition to all the various forms of *visual* pornography, there is quite a cottage industry of soft porn romance novels of varying degrees of appalling. While many Christian women would never dream of looking at visual porn, they are often far more susceptible to imaginative and emotional porn. Whether by paperback novels or sappy movies, for some reason, many otherwise thoughtful Christians are eager to indulge lustful fantasies so long as there are bonnets and hoop skirts involved, sometimes even offered with a Christian veneer of "God words" or Bible verses. While many men are trained to be bitter and discontent by their lustful viewing habits, many women are trained in the same sorts of sins—bitterness, discontentment—by their discipleship under the tutelage of Lifetime and Hallmark movies, chock full of lies about love and romance and relationships, and often deeply misandristic—resentful of true, biblical masculinity. And yes, I know that my generalizations do not apply to everyone equally: some women struggle with visual pornography and some men struggle with emotional fantasies. So keep reading.

One final word, and this is a word of grace for everyone, whatever their struggle, whatever their past. God sent His beloved Son into this sexual cesspool of a world in order to rescue filthy and failed sexual sinners. Remember what we talked about at the very beginning of this book. We are Christians. If you know Jesus, you must know Him first and foremost as your *Savior*. He did not come for the healthy, the good, the clean. He came for the sick, the wicked, and the defiled. Have you sinned sexually, either in the ways I mentioned in this chapter or in other ways? Was your sexual sin grievous and defiant or deviant? Did you know better and did you do it anyway? Did you lie, did you cheat, did you steal? Then you *qualify*. You qualify for God's grace. And this is the message of God's grace to those covered in the guilt and shame of sexual sin: I will remember your sins no more (Heb. 8:12). As far as the east is from the west, so have I have removed your sins from you (Ps. 103:12). Though your sins be like scarlet, I will wash you whiter than snow (Is. 1:18). If you confess your sins, He is faithful and just to forgive you and cleanse you from *all* unrighteousness (1 Jn. 1:9). If you have any ongoing guilt for your sexual sin, pull out your Bible right now and read those verses. Maybe read them a few times. Have you confessed your sins? Then believe the gospel, believe the good news. Christ died for your sins.

Don't say that it doesn't matter anymore, that you have failed so many times that there's nothing you can do about it. No, that's the lie of the devil, the Accuser, who is essentially saying that you can't get clean now. He's lying and saying that you are defiled, damaged goods, that you cannot ever really stand holy before a holy God or have a happy marriage under the blessing of God. No, those are lies, *damned* lies, lies from the pit of Hell. The Accuser accuses by bringing up real sins and false sins, and he doesn't mind playing dirty. All he wants is to heap up condemnation. Who is the bride of Christ? Who is the wife of our Savior? She was a whore, a prostitute, a sexually defiled tramp, defiled with all the idols of the nations (e.g., Is. 1:21, Jer. 3:1–2, Ezek. 16:15–16). And what has Christ's blood done for her? Christ's blood has washed her *clean*. "Christ also loved the church and gave Himself for her, that He might sanctify and cleanse her with the washing of water by the word, that He might present her to Himself a glorious church, not having spot or wrinkle or any such thing, but that she should be holy and without blemish" (Eph. 5:25–27, NKJV). Do you believe? Then there is therefore now no condemnation for those who are in Christ Jesus (Rom. 8:1).

Why did Jesus die? In order to cleanse the filthy, in order to take away every spot, wrinkle, and blemish. He took our condemnation so that there might be no condemnation for those who look to Him. This is the glorious story that fills the pages of Scripture: Who was Rahab? A prostitute in Jericho who turned to the God of Israel and became the mother of Boaz, the great-grandmother of David, and the ancestress of the Messiah. Who was Bathsheba? An adulteress, perhaps the victim of a political power play, and she became the mother of Solomon and the ancestress of the Messiah. Who was Abraham? A foolish man who slept with his servant girl? Yes, and the father of all the faithful. Who was David? A polygamist, an adulterer, an accomplice of murder? Yes, and a man after God's own heart. And so on. Who are you? A sinner? Yes, and an heir of eternal life, a friend of God, and no mere mortal.

So get your head and heart around this grace. Or better, let this grace get around your head and heart. The whole point of being a Christian is the fact that we are lost, we have failed, we have sinned. And Jesus is our righteousness, our goodness, our only hope. Turn to Him now, repent of your sins, be cleansed, and walk in the light. The same God who calls the light out of the darkness declares sinners clean who turn to Him in faith. No matter your past, you can walk down the aisle in purity. No matter your past, you can stand at the altar and take vows under the absolute blessing of God. And if you have already broken your marriage vows, even repeatedly, this grace is still for you—there is still hope for you. As Pastor Douglas Wilson loves to say, God meets us right where we are, not where we were supposed to be. This grace is not possible by getting your act together, by trying harder, or by reading some Christian books. This grace is only possible by faith in Christ, and in Christ alone. It's a gift to be received, and then all you do is *walk* in it.

When there has been sexual sin, there are often consequences. Sometimes there are out-of-wedlock pregnancies, past abortions, venereal diseases, bad habits, divorce, child support payments, guilt, and shame, and the gospel of grace does not magically make all of those consequences simply or instantaneously disappear. The gospel *does* immediately and judicially take away your guilt and shame, but the *feelings* of guilt and shame often take time to heal, and there may be legal, medical, financial, or relational realities that remain. But what the gospel of grace does is give you a certain hope that God can and will bless you as you walk faithfully *through* whatever consequences are before you today. There is no way *around* your sin, there is only a way through, either through on your own or through with Christ. The path through with Christ is the path of honest confession to God and all those you have sinned against. As you confess your sins to those you have sinned against, and as you take responsibility for your actions, you have an anchor for your soul that is within the veil, that links you to God in Christ (Heb. 6:19–20). What can separate you from the love of God in Christ? Nothing. Nothing at all (Rom. 8:35–39). This is the foundation of Christian life, the foundation for Christian marriage, and the only foundation for true healing and restoration.

Get clean in Christ. Walk in the joy of the Lord. Walk in His light. Tell the truth. Confess your sins. Forgive one another quickly. Take responsibility for your actions. Put things right. Cut off the hand, pluck out the eye that causes you to sin. Be good. Get married. Keep your vows. Live forever.

QUESTIONS FOR DISCUSSION

1. *What is fornication? What is adultery?*

2. *How far is too far?*

3. *Why is sexual sin before marriage bad practice for married life?*

4. *How is pornography idolatry, and how is it terrible preparation for marriage?*

5. *How does the gospel address sexual sin?*

CHAPTER 17

WHAT DO YOU THINK ABOUT...?

S o, what do you think about *everything*?
If you're going to promise to marry someone and live with them for the rest of your life, you should probably find out everything you can about them and what they think. For example, you really ought to know if you're marrying a die-hard Yankees fan or something unfortunate like that. If you've been married for a few years or many years, and you want to do some retooling, you really have the same project in front of you. If that's you, I'm sure you know by now that you still have work to do on this matter. And remember, one of the fun things about people is that some of their preferences and opinions change over time. What is their favorite thing

to do? Is it still the same as five or ten or twenty years ago? What would be an ideal getaway? How long does it take you to come up with gift ideas for Christmas or a birthday? What sorts of things do your wife or husband think about frequently? Are there things that used to be very important to them, but aren't as important any more? Or vice versa?

Okay, realistically there's no way to cover *everything*. And Christians marry *by faith*, just like we do everything else in this life. This means that you marry another person not knowing everything. There are some things that are unseen and unknown, and being a Christian means that you trust God with those things. So here's some thirty-thousand-foot advice for you engaged couples if that list of questions was starting to make you sweat: Once you confirm that you are both Christians, that you inhabit the same basic theological orbit, that you are both committed to obeying what the Bible says about the roles of husband and wife, and that you like being around one another, you're probably good to go.

But that doesn't mean that living together and loving one another will take no effort. And part of the effort it takes to live together and love one another well is the effort of communication and talking about stuff *a lot*. The point of asking the following questions and others like them is not that you can actually cover Every. Single. Thing. Neither is the point to have the *answers* to every question completely answered right this minute. The point of these questions is to begin or continue a lifelong conversation. Some answers may come easily, some maybe not so much. Some may need to be more fully answered sooner than others. But in my experience, these are the sort of things that are likely to come up at some point, and you'll need to make decisions about them. Hopefully this is a list of helpful conversation starters. Don't panic if you don't know the answers yet. Just start talking, read your Bible, pray, and seek out biblical counsel.

With that said, here is a helpful list of questions to talk about:

1. *What is the Bible? How does someone become a Christian? Who should be baptized? How important is attending church?*

I mentioned above that you should make sure that you're in the same basic theological orbit, and these are a few of the basic questions that should confirm that or at least help you understand the lay of the land. Is the Bible the very Word of God? Or is it merely an old book that generally tells you some helpful spiritual and moral advice? This is actually crucial. If the Bible is the very Word of God, then it is perfect and authoritative in all that it says, on every topic it speaks to. If God does not speak to us in the Bible, then we are just trying to figure it out on our own. The Bible itself seems very clear on this point: "All Scripture is given by inspiration of God, and is profitable for doctrine, for reproof, for correction, for instruction in righteousness, that the man of God may be complete, thoroughly equipped for every good work" (2 Tim. 3:16–17, NKJV).

What is a Christian? Is it just someone who goes to church? Is the decision to believe in Christ entirely up to each individual person's "free will"? Or does God have anything to do with it? Or does God have *everything* to do with it? These are questions that surround what theologians refer to as the Calvinist/Arminian debate. And while you certainly can be a true Christian and hold to either side (or try to straddle the sides), your convictions here will have downstream effects. My own understanding is that God is completely sovereign over the salvation of sinners. Since we were dead spiritually, we could not believe until God made us alive (Eph. 2:5–9). When God makes someone alive, He gives them the gift of faith that clings to Christ alone. A Christian is someone who believes that Jesus has died in their place, satisfying God's justice, taking away all their sins, and guaranteeing their place in Heaven with God forever. A Christian is also marked by baptism in water in the name of the Father, Son, and Holy Spirit.

Speaking of baptism, good Christians differ over who should be baptized and when and how. Should infants or young children be baptized? Only older children or adults? Should the children of believers be baptized? Should individuals be fully immersed under water, should water be poured over them, or it sufficient for a little bit of water to be sprinkled on their heads? While a husband and wife may have different views on these questions, there will come a time when there are practical decisions to be made, like when your first child is born. So it's a good idea to know where you stand and what the plan is. My first recommendation on this would be that the man know his own convictions on this matter and that a woman agreeing to marry that man be willing to follow his convictions. And if you're already married, then the same principle stands. My second recommendation is to study Scripture together carefully and know why you believe what you believe. My third recommendation is to baptize your babies when you have them on the basis of God's covenant promises. How's that for subtle? But speaking of the covenant, Christian couples should have a very high view of the covenant community, that is, being in covenant with a local body of committed believers. Finding a good church should not be an afterthought.

2. *What are your thoughts on the necessity of a Christian education for children?*

Christians coming together to form a new family must be completely committed to raising their children in the nurture and admonition of the Lord. This is because God has commanded us to do so (Deut. 6:7–9, Eph. 6:4). From just these two passages in Deuteronomy and Ephesians, we see that God requires His people to teach their children to love Him with all that they are *all day long.* This necessarily excludes the public/government educational systems and programs that are intentionally and officially dedicated to teaching children that God is irrelevant. There may be some covert operatives in some small-town public schools in this country still reading the Bible and teaching children to love God in science, history, and math all day long, but for the most part, American public schools have become the catechism classes of secularism, Darwinism, socialism, and all manner of sexual perversion. Christians should be committed to embracing the sacrifices necessary to keep their children out of public

schools and provide them an explicitly Christian education. And this will necessarily take great sacrifices of time,
energy, and money. The thing to remember here is that
our goal is not merely for our children to survive; our goal
is to see our children *thrive*. We want our children growing up sharp as arrows, mighty in God's kingdom. As we
have seen, children are some of the most potent weapons
in God's arsenal, but that doesn't happen automatically
or magically. It happens through careful, thoughtful, daily instruction. The words "nurture and admonition" literally mean "culture and counsel." God requires fathers
in particular to see to it that their children are raised in
the culture and counsel of Jesus. Churches and Christians
with more wealth should do whatever they can to come
alongside Christians with less financial means seeking to
pay for a Christian education. Lastly, not all "Christian"
schools are actually Christian or thriving spiritually. So
do your homework, meet some of the alumni, and take
this duty seriously. Don't just send your kids to the first
listing in the Google search engine that says "Christian."

3. *How do you think about health, nutrition, and
medical decisions?*

Here's another immensely practical topic where feelings can run high pretty quickly given the fact that sometimes we really are talking about life and death decisions.

For example: Will you give birth at home or the hos-
pital? Will you vaccinate or not? Are you generally trust-
ful of modern medicine, or is it grandma's magic herbal
stew for all your ailments? Are you into nutritional fads
(e.g., gluten-free, fat-free, no-hormone beef), or are you

a human garbage disposal? Or maybe somewhere in the middle? Do you eat fast food? Do you exercise? And why or why not?

Did your blood pressure rise as you read any of these questions?

Broadly speaking, it is undeniable that modern medicine has been a tremendous blessing. Life expectancy has never been as high in human history, at least since the Flood, and many of the treatments available for sicknesses and diseases that were once considered fatal are really marvelous. At the same time, this same modern medical industry is fast approaching a mass internal combustion of incoherence and insanity. The Hippocratic oath, "First, do not harm," is in great jeopardy now as abortion on demand has permeated Western culture, alongside creeping acceptance of euthanasia and so-called "transgender" mutilation. Combine this with the growing hubris and tyranny of the modern State, and there is little doubt as to why many people are fleeing for the hills, abandoning all trust in medical professionals. If you can't tell the difference between a baby and a clump of cells, why should we trust you with anything else?

At the same time, I would argue that the Bible teaches us to generally respect the ancient landmarks, that is, trust what we have learned in the past. This should not be an unquestioning trust or a naïve trust, but things like double-blind trials really are a gift to modern medical science. And there really is something significant about the rigorous testing process that modern medicines must clear. We should also definitely be aware of the fact that old wives' tales really can be problematic (1 Tim. 4:7). Likewise, "For bodily exercise profits a little, but godliness is profitable for all things, having promise of the life that now is and of that which is to come" (1 Tim. 4:8, NKJV). And do not underestimate the idols of health and nutrition. The belly gods have always been mighty to cause great divisions in families and churches (Rom. 16:17–18). Whatever your personal preferences, do not bind other peoples' consciences where God has not spoken. "But food does not commend us to God; for neither if we eat are we the better, nor if we do not eat are we the worse" (1 Cor. 8:8, NKJV). That's a really good thing to remember. Food does not commend us to God. And therefore, if God has not forbidden it, then give thanks and rejoice, and do not forbid it (1 Tim. 4:3).

Last point on this is the necessary element of faith in making your health and nutrition and medical decisions. Everyone wants to do their best to honor God with these decisions, but the fact of the matter is that we don't know everything. All we have is the information God gives us. Remember, for thousands of years it was thought that bleeding someone helped expel noxious humors from a sick body. And no doubt many a godly physician is now in Heaven, having been set straight, and he is now in full fellowship with fellow believers he helped to Heaven perhaps sooner than was medically necessary. And no doubt we will have our own foibles and misunderstandings to be set straight. Remember, being a Christian means that this life is not everything. We want to be good stewards of these bodies, but these bodies are cursed by the Fall and are dying. Our ultimate hope and goal is not to have the longest life possible. Our ultimate hope and goal is to have the longest life possible *under the blessing of God* and to be raised from the dead in new and glorious bodies. Remember the wisdom of "better than," and make sure you keep your eye on the ball. Sure, some food is better for you than other food. But joy and gratitude are better than fussiness and legalism and bitterness.

4. *How do you think about finances, debt, credit cards, tithing, and saving for retirement?*

Are you a penny-pincher? Do you have a credit card? How much do you save each month?

This is mostly a matter of planning, but as you get married, you will find that you probably have slightly different methods or preferences. And there are some basic biblical principles when it comes to personal finances. Frequently, one spouse is a bit more of a conservative saver and the other is a bit more of the liberal spender. The first biblical principle to keep in mind is the fact that the husband is the head of the wife here in the financial department. A man ought to know his own principles, and they ought to be derived from Scripture and common sense. Among them ought to be *Don't spend more than you actually have* and *The debtor is slave to the lender* (Prov. 22:7). A man who has asked a woman to marry him has asked her to let him provide for her financially. So these matters are not at all irrelevant to the proposition.

Will you carry health insurance or at least be members of some sort of Christian healthcare sharing program? When I asked my future father-in-law if I could marry his daughter, he asked me to put together a two-year monthly budget on an Excel spreadsheet (he wanted us to finish the last two years of college for our undergraduate degrees), and he told me that he would require his daughter to be covered by health insurance. In the twenty years since our marriage, my wife has been covered by health insurance of some form or other, and the cost of premiums has been repaid many times over by our medical needs over the years.

How will you budget? Who will pay the bills? Will you set a plan at the beginning of each month and review how the previous month went?

The Bible says that a good man leaves an inheritance to his children's children (Prov. 13:22). For Christians, saving for retirement should not be saving up enough money to blow on Caribbean cruises for the last three decades of your life. The goal of saving up for retirement is to not burden your children and grandchildren when you can no longer work to provide for yourself. The laziness and selfishness that has often characterized modern American retirement is a great shame. Our goal as Christians should be to work as long as we can to provide for ourselves and our immediate family, as well as our descendants. Sometimes it makes good sense to retire from one vocation at some point well before our strength is gone, but this should include a plan to continue being fruitful for the kingdom of God and providing for our own as long as the Lord gives us strength.

Part of being a Christian is also planning to be generous. Christian generosity is not just haphazard and random. When we are good stewards of the resources God gives us, we will find that there is usually more than we need for our bare necessities. Husbands should lead and provide for their families by blessing them with gifts and holidays. God did this in the wilderness with the people of Israel, requiring them to keep a weekly Sabbath and hold periodic festivals. In the New Covenant, we keep the Lord's Day as our Christian Sabbath, a weekly holiday, and men should see to it that they give rest to their wives and children on this day and on other occasions from time to time. It is not wasteful to take your family away every year to a cabin or the beach if God has provided the resources to do that. Done in the right spirit, family vacation should fall under the category of generosity, hospitality, and giving freely. You are also building a family culture, making memories, and establishing habits of fellowship and friendship that by God's blessing will last for generations. But neither should you spend what you don't have. God accepts our generosity based upon what we have, not requiring us to give what we do not have (2 Cor. 8:12). Likewise, Christians should plan to tithe on their increase to support the work of their local church as well as look for opportunities to give additional offerings to worthy ministries, Christian schools, and missionary efforts and to practice hospitality.

QUESTIONS FOR DISCUSSION

1. *Were there any questions in this chapter you haven't discussed or thought about before? Discuss them.*

2. *Which areas do you find the most challenging or difficult? What can you do to address the challenges?*

3. *Are there any other areas that were not covered in this chapter that you think need further discussion?*

4. *How are your relationships with your (future) in-laws? How are you working to honor parents and communicate expectations clearly?*

5. *Who are your most trusted counselors/advisors that you would go to for guidance in one of these areas?*

CHAPTER 18

WHAT THE BIBLE SAYS
ABOUT DIVORCE

WHILE it might seem strange or unsettling to include an entire chapter on divorce in a book about
marriage, to me that objection smacks more of sentimentalism than biblical thinking. Sentimentalism prioritizes
feelings over biblical truth. But Christians love the truth,
and we rejoice in right sentiment and the gift of emotions
in their rightful place, submitting to God.

All of that to say, there's nothing else in this world
with stakes as high as marriage where you would not
dream of having thought through the possible dangers or
outcomes. You sign medical release forms and indemnity
forms all the time. You read the warnings on the labels of
the medicines you take. Nearly all of the other significant

decisions you make in this world include fine print warnings, cautions, and full disclosures. And the Bible does the same thing with marriage. The Bible is utterly clear that marriage is between one man and one woman *for life*—what God has joined together let no man put asunder (Matt. 19:6). God hates divorce, and Malachi says that God hates divorce particularly for the way it covers people in violence (Mal. 2:16).

This may seem like an extreme way to put it, but you should think of violence in its fullest biblical sense: violent words, violent emotions, the division of a family, the tearing apart of children, siblings, parents, bank accounts, houses, futures, hearts. Violence isn't an extreme word at all for it. Divorce is violent. And this is fundamentally the case because in the marriage covenant God truly makes two people one flesh. It takes violence to break that union. So we begin with the clear conviction that what God has joined together, let no man separate. And the only *ordinary* lawful dissolution of marriage is by death. What is not lawful for man to do, God is the sovereign Lord of. He is Master of life and death, and when a spouse dies, God has sovereignly dissolved that marriage (Rom. 7:2). The remaining spouse is free to remarry if they so choose, but only in the Lord.

Yet God in His mercy also recognizes that there are some situations where the violence of sin has so damaged the covenant relationship that He grants the innocent party freedom to divorce. This is what Jesus says in the gospels: "But I say to you that whoever divorces his wife for any reason except sexual immorality causes her to commit adultery; and whoever marries a woman who is divorced commits adultery" (Matt. 5:32, NKJV, cf. 19:9). The word that Jesus uses here for "sexual immorality" is *porneas*, the word for fornication, which is why some Christians believe that Jesus is only making an exception for someone who has falsely presented themselves as a virgin *prior* to marriage, as can be seen in Deuteronomy 22:13–21. But I take Jesus to be referring here to sexual immorality in general, which is another definition of *porneas*, and while it could include failure to disclose sexual activity prior to marriage it could also include sexual immorality after the marriage covenant has been made (e.g., adultery). Some have pointed out that in Luke's gospel no exception is listed (16:18), but common rules of exegesis do not pit slight differences like this against one another. Luke's version teaches the clear point that God hates divorce, and Matthew's version does the same, while noting the exception.

So, when there has been sexual immorality—adultery, prostitution, or possibly persistent or deviant porn use—the innocent party has the option to divorce. But this decision ought to be weighed carefully and with the input of godly pastors and wise counselors. Even in these heartbreaking situations, the gospel *leans* toward forgiveness and reconciliation. Where the covenant breaker is truly sorrowful, repentant, and seeking accountability and pastoral care, I believe the general encouragement to the innocent party should be to forgive and cautiously seek reconciliation. While this process should not be drawn out unnecessarily, it should also not be done hastily and without due diligence. In some situations, the depth of depravity and habits of sin reveal a sort of double-life and habitual deception such that a spouse has virtually no way of knowing what is true or not, and reconciliation would seem humanly impossible. Other factors that may be relevant may include whether crimes have been committed and whether prison time is likely or not (e.g., rape, child porn). While it is certainly not required, the innocent party may file for divorce in such cases where the marriage covenant has been broken by sexual infidelity. And in such cases, the innocent party is free to remarry in the Lord.

The Bible also speaks to situations where one spouse is not a Christian. This may be the case because one spouse becomes a Christian while the other does not. This may also occur when a *professing* Christian is revealed to not really be a true believer after all. Paul says that if an unbelieving spouse is willing to remain married to a believer, the believer ought to gladly remain in the marriage, knowing that their presence has a sanctifying effect on the unbelieving spouse and any children they have together (1 Cor. 7:13–14). But Paul says that if an unbelieving spouse leaves a believer, the believing brother or sister is not under bondage in such cases (1 Cor. 7:15). I take this to mean that a believer is considered an innocent party in such a divorce and is therefore free to remarry in the Lord. Paul's argument is that a believer ought to remain with an unbeliever so long as the unbeliever is "willing to live" with him or her. Literally, the Greek means "pleased to dwell with," and we may combine this with Paul's concluding thought that we are called to peace. One final proviso on this sort of situation: in cases where a believer knowingly and obstinately married an unbeliever, a great deal of wisdom should be exercised by pastors. On the one hand, this exception should not be used as an easy-button escape clause for a sinful and foolish decision to marry an unbeliever. On the other hand, the mass divorce of Israelite men from their foolish marriages to foreign wives under the pastoral care of Ezra does not seem entirely irrelevant to such a situation (Ezra 10).

Another biblical text that allows for divorce and remarriage is found in Exodus 21. Moses says that if a man takes a second wife, he may not diminish the food, clothing, or sexual rights of his first wife (Exod. 21:10). But if he takes a second wife and does not fulfill his duties in this respect, the first wife is free to leave without penalty (Exod. 21:11). I take Paul's instructions to husbands to "nourish and cherish" their wives to be a reiteration of this basic principle, since "nourish and cherish" literally means "feed and keep warm" (Eph. 5:29). This is the biblical case for allowing divorce in cases of desertion or severe abuse. If we may also reason from the previous case of a marriage between a believer and an unbeliever, a man who either abandons his wife or through severe, perpetual neglect or abuse has *de facto* abandoned his wife, is not "pleased to dwell with" his wife. I would argue that in these cases, it is important for the elders of the church to make a ruling whether abandonment has occurred or when, in their judgment, a man has so severely abused or neglected his basic marital duties that a woman is free to divorce him and to remarry in the Lord.

And this is another reason, incidentally, why it should be a high priority to be members of a local church, under the authority of wise and godly elders who will both hold you accountable to God's Word and make wise judgments about difficult situations.

One final scenario that the Bible addresses is the situation where there are no biblical grounds for divorce, but a divorce is nevertheless permitted because of the hardness of hearts. This is what Jesus explained to the Pharisees: "They said to Him, Why then did Moses command to give a certificate of divorce, and to put her away? He said to them, Moses, because of the hardness of your hearts, permitted you to divorce your wives, but from the beginning it was not so" (Matt. 19:7–8, NKJV; cf. Mk. 10:5). Jesus continues in the following verse to note that remarriage to a new spouse in that scenario would constitute a form of adultery (Matt. 19:9). So Moses allowed for divorce because of the hardness of hearts, but in those situations a subsequent remarriage compounded the sin, adding adultery to the hardness of heart. Paul likewise acknowledges a scenario where divorce may occur when remarriage is not an option: "A wife is not to depart from her husband. But even if she does depart, let her remain unmarried or be reconciled to her husband. And a husband is not to divorce his wife" (1 Cor. 7:10–11, NKJV). These situations are more akin to a legal separation, which may be a wiser route to follow than divorce, but laws may vary from state to state and dictate different paths of prudence. Again, in such situations it is important that elders and pastors issue clear judgments regarding whether an individual is eligible for remarriage or not.

It's important to point out that in every one of these cases, Jesus is clear that forgiveness is always required. Offending parties are required to ask for forgiveness, and the party that has been sinned against must be ready and willing to forgive the one who sinned against them from the heart. "Then Peter came to Him and said, Lord, how often shall my brother sin against me, and I forgive him? Up to seven times? Jesus said to him, I do not say to you, up to seven times, but up to seventy times seven" (Matt. 18:21–22, NKJV). In some situations, the one who has sinned may not actually seek forgiveness, and in those situations it is impossible to close the transaction of forgiveness, but the spouse who was sinned against should still have forgiveness prepared for the one who wronged them. Forgiveness should be baking in their hearts, ready to be extended and granted as soon as the offender asks for it. You want to be like the father of the prodigal son, looking down the road for the one who sinned against you, ready to run toward them and forgive them fully when they ask.

At the same time, it should be noted that forgiveness is not the same thing as trust. A Christian businessman may catch a Christian employee embezzling money from the company, and the employee may sincerely repent and seek forgiveness, and the Christian businessman must *forgive* the employee, but the employer still has the full Christian option of firing the employee. Being an employee is not a position of Christian fellowship; it is a privileged position of blessing and honor. Likewise, "husband" is an office of privilege and honor, not a position of absolute right. When the authority and privilege of an office have been abused or the trust broken, that authority and privilege have sometimes been forfeited. In Christian marriage, God makes it clear that it is extremely hard to remove a spouse from the office of husband or wife, but it is not impossible. Forgiveness means that you accept someone as a fellow Christian in Christ. Forgiveness means that you are in fellowship at the table of the Lord. Forgiveness means that you do not hold their sin against them. But forgiveness does not require you afterward to trust them to be your wife or husband (or pastor or police officer).

Nevertheless, forgiveness is the only path of seeing clearly. The opposite of forgiveness is bitterness, and bitterness is a poison that muddles everything. You have to forgive in order to see clearly, in order to know what you ought to do in any given situation. In any Christian marriage, sin is always an act of hatred and a breach of trust, and, therefore, the gospel teaches us not only to forgive but also to love one another as we repent toward greater and greater holiness. Love covers a multitude of sins. And even in some of the most heartbreaking cases of sin and betrayal, the gospel is the only hope for healing and reconciliation. And if we have been forgiven much, our instinct ought to be to forgive much.

QUESTIONS FOR DISCUSSION

1. Why is it worth considering what the Bible teaches about divorce when preparing for marriage?

2. How does divorce cover people with violence?

3. What are the two clearest grounds for divorce in the Bible? Cite Bible verses to defend your position.

4. How would you defend from Scripture the idea that desertion or extreme mistreatment are grounds for divorce?

5. What is the difference between forgiveness and trust? When must a Christian forgive? If adultery is forgiven, may the offended spouse still file for divorce?

CHAPTER 19

A THEOLOGY OF
WEDDINGS & RECEPTIONS

IF the world is busy seeking to press us into their mold, it should not come as a surprise that they are running plays in less obvious ways all around the celebration of marriage. Christians need to remember the ancient Christian maxim *lex orandi lex credendi*, the law of prayer is the law of faith, and this just means that liturgy matters. How we pray and worship will over time teach us *how* to believe, either for better or worse. This principle is most important in formal Lord's Day worship, but it still applies to our personal and family worship as well as our lesser ceremonies, including our weddings. How we celebrate marriage, over time, teaches us how to think about marriage. If we are flippant and casual in marriage ceremonies, can there be any surprise if we are flippant and casual with our marriage vows? If we do not take our wedding vows seriously on our wedding day, why would we take them seriously five years in when things have gotten really tough or challenging? In other words, what are we practicing for?

Likewise, since Christian marriage is one of the significant ways we proclaim the gospel, surely a Christian wedding must give thought to how we will proclaim the gospel. Wherever the Lord gives us an opportunity to proclaim the gospel, we ought to do so, as far as it depends upon us, *thoughtfully*, not thoughtlessly. How does the wedding ceremony, the clothes we wear, the music we choose, and the celebration afterward proclaim the gospel of Jesus? Thoughtfulness need not mean boring or stiff or fussy. When David considered how God is mindful of man, how thoughtful He is of us, it astounded him and made him burst out in praise (Psalm 8). Thoughtfulness should be an opportunity for additional blessing and joy, not less. In what follows, I will walk through the basic biblical elements of a wedding ceremony, commenting on various elements as I do so, and then I will leave a sample wedding ceremony in the final chapter for those of you planning your wedding to consider. For those of you who are already married, whether or not all of these elements were present in your wedding ceremony, these elements are present in the substance of every Christian marriage.

First, what is a wedding? A wedding is a covenant ceremony in which vows are taken and witnessed with the result that one man and one woman become one flesh and form a new family (Gen. 2:18, 24). In its bare bones, you simply need a man and a woman taking marriage vows, witnesses to those vows, and, afterward, the consummation of the marriage through sexual union. Since marriage is a creation ordinance, it is an institution into which all human beings may enter by virtue of creation, so long as it abides by these most basic creational standards. For this reason, a marriage could be contracted by two families in somebody's backyard if they wanted. It would be a real marriage. But like the apostle Paul, we might say that while all things may be lawful, not all things are necessarily edifying. We are not merely interested in what the bare minimum is. Knowing Christ, living for Christ, means living for His blessing, wanting to see His blessing on us, our families, our neighbors—we want His blessing to the fill the whole earth. So a pox on bare minimums! We are Christians. We love the abundance of God's grace, the gratuity of the gospel. It's over the top, lavish, extravagant. And God loves it when His people celebrate His abundance. It magnifies His grace. While it may be said that our modern culture is happy to lure people into materialistic folly, running up credit cards in order to have a wedding that looks like something out of the magazines and movies, it must also be said that the devil would also like nothing more than Christians to be stingy and prudish and grumpy about celebrating God's abundance. So, without bowing to the materialistic gods, Christians must also resolutely defy the utilitarian gods and gnostic gods. Christians must seek to celebrate a wedding like Christians, which means with a high and dignified joy, with a great generosity and abundance, measured to what God has actually given us (2 Cor. 8:12). For some, this will mean pulling out your best slacks and nicest dress and having friends and family pitch in to throw the best backyard ceremony and party you can. And praise God for that! For others, it might mean a tuxedo and a new dress in a stately old church, but whatever it is, let it be a sacrifice of praise, let it be within your actual means, and let it be your best. And of course, there should be some really good wine (Jn. 2:1–11).

For Christians, marriage is not merely a *contract,* because embedded in the creation of marriage is a glorious and mysterious sign of the gospel: "'Therefore a man shall leave his father and mother and hold fast to his wife, and the two shall become one flesh.' This mystery is profound, and I am saying that it refers to Christ and the church" (Eph. 5:31–32). While the Roman Catholic tradition has wrongly elevated marriage to a sacrament in part based on this verse, the Reformation tradition that I am part of has rightly affirmed that marriage is a *covenant* blessed by God. A covenant is a bond formed around promises with attendant blessings and curses. The gospel is the offer of the New Covenant in which all Christians participate by faith in Christ, sealed by baptism. While marriage does not participate in the New Covenant formally, it is a reflection or a type of that covenant, a sign that points to it, which God promises to be present for and to work His blessing in.

This is why the old instinct to have our Christian weddings in a church, or at least having a minister of the gospel officiating the service, makes good sense. While marriage is properly under the jurisdiction of the government of the family, the governments of the Church and state have a legitimate interest in who gets married to whom. The Church has a moral jurisdiction to make sure the two parties are morally eligible to be married and to hold the parties to their vows and to pastor the family through life. The state has a civil interest in weddings related to protecting property and inheritance, and, in the event of a death or divorce, to protect justice for all parties involved. This is why in many Christian lands a wedding is performed by a minister (often in a church) with a marriage license filed with the county for civil recordkeeping.

While not required, it makes sense for Christians that in some ways a wedding ceremony would reflect elements of our worship service (e.g., Christian prayers and hymns, Scripture reading, an exhortation from Scripture, and a benediction). In the Puritan tradition (my tradition), there was so much concern to avoid Roman Catholic superstition that weddings were once not permitted to be separate ceremonies but were rather included as part of a formal worship service, often on a Sunday evening. Since in those days there was such concern about extra-biblical ceremonies creeping in, the Puritans wanted to worship God by obeying only explicit commands (what is known as the Regulative Principle of Worship). Since the Psalms spoke of "vows" being paid to the Lord as acts of worship, they concluded that a couple might take their marriage vows before God and the congregation. While

I don't think this extra caution is necessary, I do think that Protestant Christians should take care that the wedding ceremony reflects a simple but thoughtful covenant theology. The fact that a wedding is a covenant-making ceremony that seeks God's blessing and seeks to point to the gospel of the New Covenant should be clear and obvious. A Protestant wedding is not a sacramental service under the jurisdiction of the Church, but neither is it an open mic night at the local comedy club.

This covenantal conviction should also be seen in the joyful solemnity of the wedding ceremony. Wedding vows are sworn before God and before witnesses, and because God requires that we take our vows very seriously, the ceremony should have dignity. The practice of wearing nice suits and nice dresses is meant to signify that this event is a serious joy. It's glad and thankful and solemn. And when we do this in the name of Christ, a Christian wedding ceremony proclaims the serious joy of the gospel. Casual and silly antics, pop music, and trendy clothing or hair styles tend to trivialize the event, sort of like wearing flip flops and a T-shirt to a fancy dinner or to meet the president. Such trendy oddities tend to cheapen the whole event and turn the focus of the ceremony on the wedding party rather than being a glorious sign of gratitude which points to Christ.

I remember one wedding ceremony I witnessed in which there was a ceremonial smashing of the cell phones with hammers (the couple had spent months only conversing over the phone, and now that was over). While it was no doubt well-intentioned, and it certainly was not sinful, these sorts of choose-your-own-adventure "cere-monies" are really indications that we have collectively forgotten what a wedding ceremony is. Despite our cul-ture's insistence to the contrary, the marriage ceremony is not "your special day" or "all about you." The bride and groom are rightly at the center of the event, but a Christian bride and groom should want to point back to their parents and siblings and friends in gratitude and ul-timately back to their Lord Jesus for His grace and good-ness. At the same time, a wedding ceremony really should be joyful, not dry, and should be full of *blessing*—songs and prayers and toasts and benedictions should fill the ceremony and tumble out into the celebration following.

Our modern wedding ceremony is actually the com-bination of both what was historically called a "betroth-al" and the marriage ceremony proper. In the ancient world, betrothal was a legally binding promise to marry made by both parties, in which breaking the contract re-quired a divorce and unfaithfulness to it was considered adultery (e.g., Deut. 22:23–24, Matt. 1:18–25). This is because in agrarian cultures money was largely located in material property, land, harvest, etc. While our mod-ern day engagements do approach some of these factors (reserving a wedding venue, inviting guests, planning a honeymoon, etc.), the legal and material investments were considerable in the ancient world and took a fair bit of time to arrange and a great deal of personal and financial risk was involved, and so a betrothal was a le-gally binding engagement. The period of time between the betrothal and marriage varied, but it was the period of time needed to make the necessary arrangements for the new family to be formed.

In Genesis 24, we see all of the essential elements of a wedding: Abraham's servant explains his mission to find a wife for his master's son (Isaac) to Rebekah and her brother and father. "Then Laban and Bethuel answered and said, '... Behold, Rebekah is before you; take her and go, and let her be the wife of your master's son, as the LORD has spoken'" (Gen. 24:50–51, ESV). "Her brother and her mother said ... 'Let us call the young woman and ask her, "Will you go with this man?"' She said, 'I will go.' So they sent away Rebekah their sister ... And they blessed Rebekah ... [And returning] Rebekah lifted her eyes, and when she saw Isaac ... she took her veil and covered herself. And the servant told Isaac all the things that he had done. Then Isaac brought her into the tent of Sarah his mother and took Rebekah, and she became his wife, and he loved her" (Gen. 24:55–60, 64–67, ESV). We see familial permission granted, we see the woman's own vow and agreement to marry, the groom's agreement (vow) to take this woman, blessings on the event, and finally the consummation of the marriage.

During the early and medieval Church, there was rather widespread confusion concerning marriage, creating a culture where at least three competing notions swirled around: an unbiblical suspicion of the sinfulness or impurity of the married state (particularly sexual relations), an individualistic and contractual view of marriage, and a growing consensus that marriage (if it had to be entered into) was (or needed to be) a sacrament to somehow deal with the "sinful" sexual element. Thus, by the High Middle Ages, a man and woman who suddenly promised to get married and then slept together were considered married "in the sight of God," even though there had been no ceremony. Just imagine the chaos.

The Reformers set about reforming this situation such that betrothal came to serve as a waiting period during which the couple was required to remain chaste and in which the community might weigh in on the proposal. Thus, in the traditional wedding ceremony, there are usually opening (betrothal) vows (e.g., "Will you take this woman …? "I will"). Following this, the minister often asks if anyone knows of any reason why this man and woman should not be married. While it is certainly still lawful to ask that question during the ceremony, our modern day engagement announcements, social media, and prayer lists serve the same purpose of letting the public know of the intentions of the couple and inviting any questions or objections to be raised. If somebody happens to know that Joe Smith is actually still married to Susie Q down in Kentucky, somebody really should speak up *before* the actual wedding ceremony.

But all of this serves to highlight the important role that the community plays in forming new families. As we already noted, there are multiple interested parties when it comes to a wedding. The bride and groom themselves have the responsibility to voice their own consent and swear their own vows. The families of the bride and groom have interest in the event by their love, care, and responsibility before God for their son and daughter, not to mention grandchildren and inheritance concerns. The covenant community of the Church also has interest by virtue of their love and care for this brother and sister in Christ. In its most basic sense, all we mean by "courtship" is that a man and woman thinking about marriage ought to do so with the input of their families and Christian community. And where a biological family is lacking, there are many brothers and sisters, mothers and fathers in Christ, and it may be wise for singles in that situation to seek out an older man or woman or couple to mentor them.

All of this is why most wedding ceremonies usually begin by escorting principle members of the families to seats of honor (parents, grandparents). This is also why the bride is escorted by her father and accompanied by her attendants, why the groom is likewise attended by groomsmen, and why we specifically ask, "Who gives this woman to be married to this man?" This is why there has also often been a question to the entire congregation regarding their commitment and ongoing role in the life of this new family. "Will you all uphold this couple in their marriage vows?" By standing up with the couple, by escorting, and by making public vows, we are saying that a Christian marriage takes place and is blessed in the context of a covenant community. And this is because every successful marriage and family is a result of the encouragement, counsel, prayer, hospitality, generosity, examples, and admonitions of the Body of Christ.

Speaking of which, thought should also be given to the reception: it should certainly be full of joyful music, dancing, toasts, and feasting, but it should also seek to *include* and bless the community as much as possible. Just as the ceremony is not all about the couple but rather an opportunity to make vows in a context of deep gratitude to family and friends, all pointing to the goodness of God, so too a reception should continue that same spirit. If I may be permitted to put on an old man "boomer" hat for just a moment, I would encourage couples to give thought in particular for how they will bless the parents and grandparents and old folks at the reception. This may be as simple as giving consideration to making sure that stories and toasts can be heard clearly or making sure there is designated seating closer to the festivities or making sure that the music is not so loud that your most honored guests cannot hear. While I do not think this means that all of your dance music needs to be taken from the 1950s, Christian couples should not merely pick all of their modern favorites. Thinking about the children that may be attendance can be another way you give thought to the people who are there to celebrate with you. If a marriage is a celebration of God's goodness to a covenant community, give thought to how you will demonstrate that not only in the ceremony but also in the reception that follows.

There are many stages of life represented in the covenant community, each bringing with it different temptations with regard to weddings. But the central point I want to make is that weddings are not really in the first instance about *you—the couple*. Even from the very first wedding, it has always been about Christ and His love for His bride, the Church (Eph. 5:32). This is the central thing. When we've been living in glory for a million years, our particular stories will be faint, brief blinks in time, but Christ will be everything. And that is the secret to being faithful now, whether old or young, happy or disappointed, about to be married, or married for many years: a wedding proclaims the love of Christ for His bride that will never grow old, never fail, and never fade away. It all points to an immortal God with an immortal love who has shared that love with us, people who by His grace are no mere mortals. I pray that your marriage will always be marked by that solemn joy.

QUESTIONS FOR DISCUSSION

1. *What is a wedding ceremony? Given what it is, how does that affect what your wedding will be like?*

2. *What does it mean that a marriage is a "covenant" relationship?*

3. *How does the story of Rebekah broadly trace the essential elements of a wedding?*

4. *Who are the principle interested parties in a marriage ceremony? List what their legitimate interests are.*

5. *How does understanding a wedding ceremony and reception as involving the whole "covenant community" impact how you celebrate at the reception? Are there specific ways you will show honor to older or younger folks at your wedding/reception?*

CHAPTER 20

A SAMPLE WEDDING
CEREMONY

P RELUDE and Seating of Guests
      Seating of Family and Processional

Minister's Welcome:
Welcome in the Name of the Father, Son, and Holy
Spirit, Amen!

[Congregation may be seated.]

Traditional Explanation of Marriage [Optional]:
Dearly beloved: We have come together in the presence of God to witness and bless the joining together of
this man and this woman in the covenant of marriage.

The bond and covenant of marriage was established by God in creation, and our Lord Jesus Christ adorned this manner of life by His presence and first miracle at a wedding in Cana of Galilee. It signifies to us the mystery of the union between Christ and His Church, and Holy Scripture commends it to be honored among all people. The union of husband and wife in heart, body, and mind is intended by God for their mutual joy; for the help and comfort given one another in prosperity and adversity; and, God willing, for the procreation of children and their nurture in the knowledge and love of the Lord. Therefore, marriage is not to be entered into unadvisedly or lightly, but reverently, deliberately, and in accordance with the purposes for which it was instituted by God.

Opening Prayer [Optional]:

Let us pray: Almighty and ever-blessed God, whose presence is the happiness of every condition, and whose favor hallows every relation: we beseech you to be present and favorable unto these, Your servants, that they may be truly joined in the honorable estate of marriage, in the covenant of their God. As You have brought them together by Your providence, sanctify them by Your Spirit, giving them a new frame of heart fit for their new estate, enrich them with all grace, so that they may enjoy the comforts, undergo the cares, endure the trials, and perform the duties of life together as becomes Christians, under Your heavenly guidance and protection, through our Lord Jesus Christ, Amen.

Vows of Intent:

[Groom], will you have this woman to be your wedded wife, to live together after God's ordinance in the holy estate of matrimony? Will you love her, comfort her, honor, and cherish her in sickness and in health; and forsaking all others, keep yourself only for her, so long as you both shall live?

Answer: I will.

[Bride], will you have this man to be your wedded husband, to live together after God's ordinance in the holy estate of matrimony? Will you love him, comfort him, honor, and obey him in sickness and in health; and forsaking all others, keep yourself only for him, so long as you both shall live?

Answer: I will.

Will all of you witnessing these promises do all in your power to uphold this man and woman in their marriage? If so, answer by saying, "Amen."

Who gives this woman to be married to this man?
Answer: I do. [Or: her mother and I do.]

Congregational Hymn:

[Another hymn/psalm may be inserted between the Prayer of Blessing and Scripture reading, between multiple Scripture readings, or after the Exhortation if more hymns are desired.]

Prayer of Blessing for the Couple [Optional]:

[May be offered by the pastor or offered by a grand-father, father, uncle, etc., or another elder/pastor]

Scripture Reading:

[May be read by the pastor, a grandfather, father, un-cle, etc., or another elder/pastor—and there may be more than one reading if desired.]

Reader: This is the Word of the Lord!

People: Thanks be to God!

Sermon/Exhortation to Bride and Groom

Marriage Vows:

Repeat after me [Groom]: I take you [Bride], to be my wedded wife, to have and to hold from this day forward, for better for worse, for richer for poorer, in sickness and in health, to love and to cherish, till death do us part, according to God's commandments.

Repeat after me [Bride]: I take you [Groom], to be my wedded husband, to have and to hold from this day for-ward, for better for worse, for richer for poorer, in sick-ness and in health, to love, cherish, and obey, till death do us part, according to God's commandments.

Exchange of Rings:

[Groom], repeat after me: With this ring I thee wed: In the name of the Father, and of the Son, and of the Holy Spirit, Amen.

[Bride]: With this ring I thee wed: In the name of the Father, and of the Son, and of the Holy Spirit, Amen.

The Lord's Prayer [Optional]

Final Prayer of Blessing [Optional]:
(The minister may place his hand on the joined hands of the new couple):
O Eternal God, Creator and Preserver of all mankind, Giver of all spiritual grace, the Author of everlasting life, send Your blessing upon these Your servants, this man and this woman, whom we bless in Your name, that they, living faithfully together, may surely perform and keep the vow and covenant made between them, and may ever remain in perfect love and peace together, and live according to Your laws, through Jesus Christ our Lord, Amen.

Declaration of Marriage:
Inasmuch as [Groom and Bride] have covenanted together to be husband and wife before God and this company of witnesses, it is my privilege to declare that they are man and wife, in the name of the Father, and of the Son, and of the Holy Spirit, Amen.

Those whom God has joined together, let no man put asunder.

[Groom], you may kiss your bride.

Benediction:

The peace of God which passes all understanding, keep your hearts and minds in the knowledge and love of God, and of His Son Jesus Christ, our Lord; and the blessing of Almighty God: the Father, the Son, and the Holy Spirit, be upon all of you, and remain with you always, Amen!

Presentation of the new couple:

It is my great pleasure to present to you for the very first time: Mr. and Mrs. _____.

Recessional

QUESTIONS FOR DISCUSSION

1. What are your thoughts about this suggested ceremony? Are there are any elements you like or dislike? Are you comfortable with the vows? Discuss.

2. Who will be officiating your ceremony? Does he have a "usual" ceremony he uses for weddings? If so, have you looked at it and discussed it?

3. What family members/grandparents will be involved in your ceremony? Who will stand up with you (bridesmaids/groomsmen)? Will there be others involved in reading Scripture or praying?

4. Have you given thought to the music you will use for the prelude, processional, any hymns or congregational singing, and recessional? What are hoping to communicate with those selections? Do the selections match your goals?

5. Are there any other elements you were hoping or planning to include in your ceremony?